NEW 3 RD EDITION!

Three Minutes to™
Blues, Rock, and Folk Harmonica

VISIT US! BLUESHARP.COM

by David Harp

I dedicate this book to my father, Fred — a New York city firefighter — and to all of his comrades, living and dead, who have sacrificed their own safety to make "The City" a safer place for the rest of us. Also to my mother, Frieda — poet, nurse, deep spirit — without whom Fred could not have done his job, nor I mine.

Book and CD: ISBN 978-0918321-88-6
Book, CD, and Harmonica: ISBN 978-0918321-89-3

© David Harp's musical i press, 2007

Illustrated by Katie Feldman

Recording by Gus Zeising   **Anatomical Diagrams by Don Mayne**

Thanks to Lily for her Song Help   Thanks to Rita for Everything

A Few Other Books by David Harp

- Blues & Rock Harmonica Made Easy • The Three Minute Meditator*
- Music Theory Made Easy • The Pocket Harmonica Songbook • Instant Flute
- Three Minutes to Blues Harmonica: The Video • Metaphysical Fitness*
- Bending the Blues • Instant Guitar • Country & Western Harmonica Made Easy
- Music Theory Made Easy for Harmonica • Instant Blues Harmonica (Vol. I & II)
- Instant Chromatic Harmonica • The Instant Harmonica Kit for Kids
- How To Whistle Like A Pro • Make Me Musical: Instant Harmonica
- The Three Minute Meditator CD* • Me and My Harmonica
- How To Save Your Back, Neck, & Shoulders In Ten Minutes A Day • EarthCards
- The New Three Minute Meditator* • Instant Harmonica for Kids (Video)
- The Instant Rhythm Kit • How to Fight a Cold...
- Neural Path Therapy: How to Change Yo[...]n

(written with my beloved twin [...]*

D0746388

List of Songs and Solos

Table of Contents

This book is divided into "tracks." Each track of the book corresponds to one track of the CD — this book is not meant to be used by itself!

(So if you don't have the CD, please go to page 93 now.)

Read This First: Listen and Learn!

This method is actually based more on learning by listening, than on learning by reading. So feel free to read only the "Boxed" sections on pages 5 and 6, then put this book aside right now and start listening to the recording. You can just come back and glance at the book when you *hear* me suggest it.

New to harmonica? Check out the "Harmonica Care" section on page 90. It'll lengthen life — of the harmonica, at least!

Track 1: Introduction

Hi! I'm David Harp. For many years, I considered myself tone-deaf — until I learned to play the harmonica, that is. Now, playing Blues, rock, and folk "harp" has become an important and incredibly satisfying part of my daily life.

Although most of my formal training is in the field of cognitive psychology — the study of how the brain processes information — I've also taught more than half a million people to blow their blues away. By doing this over many years, through private lessons, large group workshops, books, and recordings, I've developed what I believe is the fastest and easiest harmonica method ever. And you're looking at it!

I also believe that harmonica — combined with time-tested psychological tools — is a wonderful way to reduce stress and enhance mental alertness, as I teach in workshops for corporate, governmental, and non-profit groups around the nation.

Three Minutes to Harmonica? Skeptical?

Before I learned to play, if someone had told me that I could learn to play even a little bit of harp in just three minutes, I'd have called them a liar (unless they were lots bigger than me). In fact, it took me about thirty hours of practice to play my first feeble version of a folk song, and six months of daily playing to learn even the most elementary of Blues "riffs."

So perhaps you wonder how I can teach people to play in just a few minutes. But if you can breathe in and breathe out when you want to, and feed yourself safely with a fork, you already have most of the *physical* skills that you're going to need. And I'll provide the mental and musical ones.

How to Use This Method

Some people prefer to learn by reading, others by listening. I've got both strategies covered in this method, but you will have to do some of each!

Most of the information you need is on the recording. But certain things — like learning to hold the harmonica — are easier to learn by looking than by listening. You're welcome if you like, to read every word on every page. But for fastest results, simply listen to the recording and take a peek at this book whenever you hear me suggest it. You can always come back later and read those sections that most interest you.

> For your convenience, I'll put the most crucial written information inside a box like this, so it will stand out.
>
> To keep the material organized, both the book and the recording are divided into *"Tracks."* The written material in Track 1 of the book relates to Track 1 of the recording, and so on.

> In general: any time you want or need more
> details about something you've heard on the
> recording, turn to the same track number in
> this book. Need help with the Chicago Blues
> Breathing Pattern in Track 4 of the recording?
> Just turn to Track 4 of the book, and check out
> the notation for it!

This way, if you *don't* choose to read every word, just look at
each picture and check out the boxes. There won't be too
many boxes, since almost everything that's truly important to
know is already on the recording — with one exception!

The Song Sections

What's the exception? If you want to be able to play *lots* of
songs, you'll need to use "The Song Sections!" The recording
will help you play some songs, and in the Song Sections I'll
provide you with many more in a variety of styles, all written
out in my incredibly easy to use harmonica notation system.

Useful or Interesting Stuff at the End of the Book

Here I include some information, like the instructions on
harmonica care, which is useful for everyone. Other parts,
like how to play along with other people, will be of interest to
some. For those few who may be curious, I describe my
various projects, ranging from corporate speaking to *pro bono*
efforts to aerobic harmonica enhancement, and of course
including my Red, White, & the Blues Harmonica™ work.

Enough Reading for Now

Now stop reading, turn on the CD, and go on to Track Two,
my famous "3 Minute Harmonica Lesson"! It'll teach you
everything you need to know to begin enjoying the most
entertaining, creative, satisfying hobby I've ever encountered!

Track 2: 3 Minutes to Harmonica

This is the most important track in the book and recording. It contains all the basic harmonica skills that you'll need to get started. I'll keep it short and simple. Please listen to the CD and just look at the pictures and the boxed sections in the book.

> Note: Some people like to wash their harp before playing it for the first time (page 90).

Take a Good Look

Your harmonica should have ten holes, with a number from one to ten above each hole, and a little letter "C" on it. (This means you have a harmonica in "the key of C" — page 91.) If yours *doesn't* look *more or less* like this, please go to page 93 now.

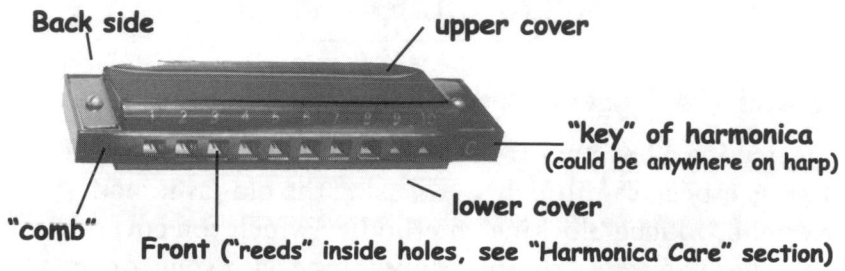

Back side

upper cover

"key" of harmonica
(could be anywhere on harp)

lower cover

"comb"

Front ("reeds" inside holes, see "Harmonica Care" section)

How to Hold Your Harmonica: The "Fork Hold"

You've been practicing this for years, every time you eat or write! Just make sure that the holes are facing your mouth (duh!) and that the little numbers are on top.

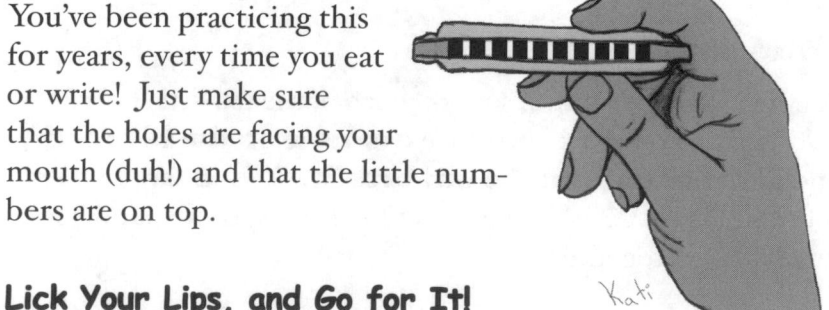

Kati

Lick Your Lips, and Go for It!

Breathe in and out through your harmonica. Lick your lips (to reduce friction) and slide around. Play the low number holes and the high ones, like I do on the recording.

The Biggest Beginner's Mistake...

...is not having the harmonica deep enough inside your mouth! Don't be afraid to eat the "tin sandwich" — cover at least three holes at a time. That's a normal and comfortable mouth open position, just like when we are talking.

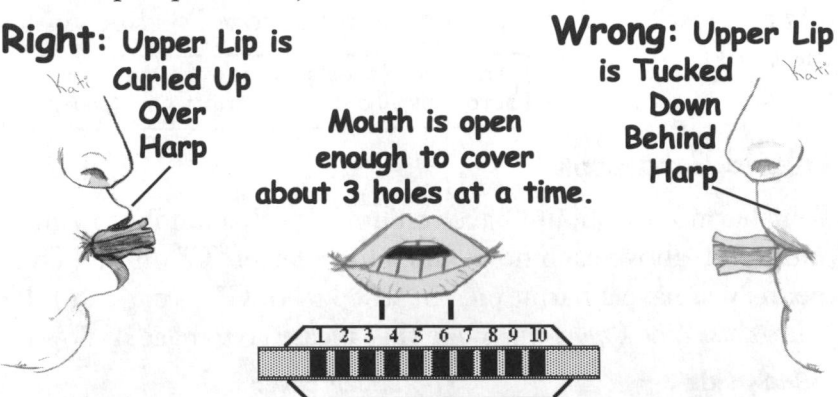

Right: Upper Lip is Curled Up Over Harp

Mouth is open enough to cover about 3 holes at a time.

Wrong: Upper Lip is Tucked Down Behind Harp

...And the Biggest Harmonica Teacher's Mistake

...is making a beginner try to play one single hole at a time. This is especially difficult to do using the old-fashioned German "tongue blocking" method, in which you cover four holes with your mouth, then cover three with your tongue. As the gangsters say, "Fagedaboutit!" Because getting single holes is the least important part of beginning to play harmonica.

Notes and Chords

A note is a single musical sound. Each of the ten little holes on your harmonica will produce **one note on the in breath,** and **another note on the out breath.** *"Chords"* are two or more notes that are "in harmony" — that is, they sound good when played together.

In fact, our instrument is called the harmonica ("harmony-ca") because the notes are always in harmony — no matter how many we play at one time. Even if you cover five or six holes with your mouth and breathe, you'll get a great sounding chord.

Ready! Aim! Play a Chord on Holes 4, 5, and 6!

Now you're ready to play along with my verbal instructions. I'll tell you which holes to aim your mouth at, when to breathe in, and when to breathe out. It's as simple as that!

Just aim your slightly opened mouth at the hole numbers that I describe. Don't worry too much about which holes you are covering — the timing of the in and out breaths are the most important thing!

Don't worry at all about playing one hole at a time — we'll mostly be playing *"chords"* (three holes at a time). So if I name three holes (like 4, 5, and 6), just aim your mouth at the middle one of the three numbers (the 5 hole). If your mouth is slightly open, the 4 hole and the 6 hole will be covered, too. For example, try playing these chords right now:

in chord on **456**   **out** chord on **456**
  (Inhale)   (Exhale)

If you like, spend a few seconds using the tip of your tongue to explore the size of the holes of the harmonica and the dividers between them. Using your tongue will help you control how many holes you cover, and help you center your mouth on the hole you want.

The Beauty of Breathing Patterns

They're easy, and they work. I believe that my Breathing Pattern method of teaching is the fastest way to get a total beginner to play Blues and rock music on the harmonica.

Why do they work so well? Because these Breathing Patterns approximate the notes of the *"Blues Scale,"* upon which most Blues and rock music is based. But don't worry about that — it's advanced music theory stuff that you don't need for now!

Steady Beat and the "Count of Four"

This is easier to hear than to read about. The "Count" helps you be ready to start playing at exactly the right time. In this case, we'll use a "Count of Four." This means that you'll start playing when you would expect me to say the word "five." Some styles of music use a count of three, or five, as you'll see.

Your First Breathing Pattern: "In—Out—In—Silence"

Try to tap your foot as you play — it'll help you to maintain a steady beat even when not playing (like during the "silent" beat).

in   out   in   (silent beat)   Empty Your Lungs Right Before Starting on an "in" Breath!

in   out   in   (silent beat)   This exercise begins at approximately 2:40 of Track Two

Keep your harmonica *way* in between your lips when playing.

Don't let air escape through nose when playing.

Don't worry about getting single holes, just aim your lips at the numbers I ask you to play.

Make sure you understand Breathing Patterns, or go back and practice them more.

Need extra help with this? Go to Track 7 of CD.

Track 3: Blues, Rock, or Folk?

If you can play the In-Out-In-Silence Breathing Pattern from Track Two, you're ready for anything! (If you can't, go back to Track Two and practice breathing with me for a few minutes, or up to Track Seven for some extra help.)

Like Blues music? Go straight to Track Four for a simple but satisfying Chicago-Style Blues *"Riff"* — based on a Breathing Pattern, of course.

> What's a riff? Just a short combination of notes or chords that we like, and memorize. Then we can use it again and again. Most of the riffs that I'll teach you are based on my Breathing Patterns.

Prefer rock and roll? Go to Track Five, and learn a Breathing Pattern for the "Boogie Woogie" riff, a foundation upon which literally thousands of rock songs are based.

Or go to Track Six, for your first actual song. This will help prepare you to play any and all of the folk, country, and classical songs that you'll find on the CD and in the Song Sections of this book.

But before you make your choice as to what to do, I'd like to offer two comments:

> This method is organized so that you can learn only the styles of music that you like best. But: 1) Learning Blues and rock music will teach you breath control that will help you to play better folk music, and 2) Learning folk music will teach you note control that will help you to play better Blues and rock...

The Easiest Notation System

You don't *need* to learn my harmonica notation system now, even though it will only take a minute to do so. But later on, when you're working with more advanced songs and riffs, it's likely to come in very handy...

Yes, you can learn a song or riff just by listening to it on the CD. But being able to see what it looks like written down can be a big help, especially for those who are visual learners.

Fortunately, I won't make you learn the musical language known as "standard notation" — that complicated-looking written music composed of lots of little lines full of funny-shaped notes and strange words.

Instead, my notation system is so simple that you've just about learned it already, simply by playing along with my vocal instructions on the recording in Track Two. It's based on three elements: Which Holes to Cover, Whether to Breathe In or Breathe Out, and How Long to Play it For...

Which Hole Numbers to Cover?

I'll write down the hole numbers that I want you to cover with your mouth. If I write down the numbers four, five, and six — you put your mouth over those holes (not too complex, is it?). A line under the numbers reminds you to play them all at the *same time*, as a chord.

The <u>456</u> Chord

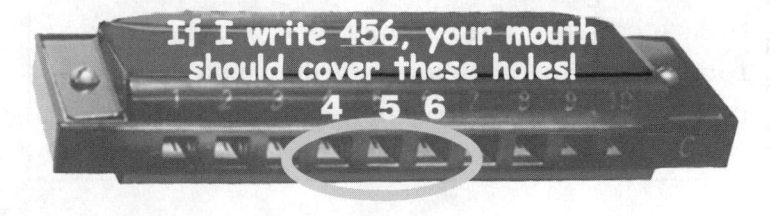

If I write <u>456</u>, your mouth should cover these holes!

Breathe In or Breathe Out?

If I want you to breathe out, I'll write the numbers in outlined type. If I want you to breathe in, I'll write the numbers in **filled in** type. So...

3̲4̲5̲ means breathe out on holes 3, 4, and 5.

1̲2̲3̲ means breathe in on holes 1, 2, and 3.

How Long to Play it For?

One Beat

I'll show you how long to hold each beat for, just as I did in Track Two when I taught you your first breathing pattern. But instead of using little foot cartoons, I'll use *dots,* to keep it simple. **Each dot** represents **one beat.**

Putting It Together...

Here's the In-Out-In-Silence Breathing Pattern on the holes four, five, and six from Track Two, in my notation.

> •   •   •   •
> **4̲5̲6̲**   4̲5̲6̲   **4̲5̲6̲** (silent beat)
>
> Numbers tell you which holes to cover with your mouth.
>
> A line under two or more numbers reminds you to play them all at the same time (as a chord).
>
> Each dot • represents one beat.
>
> outlined means breathe *out*.
>
> **filled in** means breathe *in*.
>
> If you can read the In-Out-In-Silence Breathing Pattern just above, you've got it!

Track 4: The Chicago Blues Breathing Pattern

As I introduce this track you'll hear my guitarist and me in the background, playing a style of music called the *"Twelve Bar Blues."* I sing it, too (sorry!). The guitar provides the structure, based on a specific series of guitar chords played with a Blues rhythm. Doing this is often called *"playing a chord structure,"* or *"playing a chord progression."* I add a harmonica solo "on top of" his chord structure, consisting of six versions of what I call the Chicago Breathing Pattern riff — which you'll soon learn.

> The *Twelve Bar Blues* is the most popular blues "chord structure," and is used in lots of rock, jazz and pop music, too.

You may want to listen to us a few times, just to get the feel of it. Interested in music theory, guitar, or plan to play with other musicians? If so, read this page again, then eventually see page 92 to learn the chords of the Twelve Bar Blues.

The Chicago Blues Breathing Pattern

I've developed a Breathing Pattern that works beautifully with many styles of music, although I originally began using it to teach my students to play simple harp riffs in the style of Chicago Blues musicians. I'll write it out for you: first as the general Breathing Pattern (just ins and outs), then as you'd play it on the holes four, five, and six. Make the breathing changes from in to out to in nice and crisp, and start empty!

innnn out in (three silent beats)

456 456 456 (three silent beats)

Your First Chicago Twelve Bar Blues Verse

This riff is eight beats long (counting the three silent beats). Blues musicians often refer to four beats of music as *"one bar."* So it could also be called a "two bar" riff.

> Practice playing the Chicago Riff a few times. Then play it six times along with my Blues background music, to form one *"verse"* of a Twelve Bar Blues!

It's not a great solo (kind of repetitive), but played along with a good Blues band and a big amplifier, it wouldn't sound bad!

Movin' It Around!

What's the best thing about my Breathing Pattern method? Once you learn the pattern, you can use it anywhere!

Demonstrate this for yourself by playing the Chicago Breathing Pattern on the holes 5, 6, and 7. Then on holes 6, 7, and 8. Then (although a bit shrill for most tastes), on holes 8, 9, and 10. You now know four different Chicago Blues Riffs!

• • •	•	•	• • •
567	567	**567**	**(three silent beats)**
• • •	•	•	• • •
678	678	**678**	
• • •	•	•	• • •
8910	8910	**8910**	

In the second verse, you won't just repeat the same riff six times. Instead, you'll form a more varied twelve bar solo by putting together three different riffs. As with the first verse, you'll play a two bar (eight beat) riff six times to form this second twelve bar (48 beat) blues verse.

Your Second Chicago Blues Verse

You'll use the Chicago Breathing Pattern on holes 4, 5, and 6, and on holes 6, 7, and 8, and on holes 8, 9, and 10. Don't forget the silent beats — they're an important part of the riff!

I'll talk you right through this verse using vocal instructions:

Start the verse "in the middle" by playing the 456 riff twice.

Then you'll go "a couple holes higher," and play the Chicago riff once, somewhere around the 678 holes.

Then play the 456 Chicago riff (in the middle) again, once.

Take it "Way up high!" and play the 8910 Chicago riff once.

End the verse by playing the Chicago riff once more "back in the middle," on (or around) the 456 holes.

Don't worry about exactly which holes you're on — just feel the beat and give it a try. I'm very forgiving, and so is the harmonica! Pull out your harmonica and play this solo along with your neighbor's garage band, and your friends who never heard you play before will be very impressed indeed!

Singing the Blues

Would you like to make up and sing your own blues? Listen to my example at the beginning of Track 4. You'll hear that you can fit three beats worth of lyrics into each riff (during the three silent beats).

• • • • •   •   •   •
(Chicago Riff) Now sing the Blu - ues

• • • • •   •   •   •
(Chicago Riff) Whatcha got to loo - ose

• • • • •   •   •   •
(Chicago Riff) Now Sing the Blu - ues

• • • • •   •   •
(Chicago Riff) Got noth-in' to loo - ose

• • • • •   •   •   •
(Chicago Riff) All ya need to fi - ind

• • • • •   •   •   •   •
(Chicago Riff) Is two words that rhyme!

The dots above the words I sang show you how I fit the lyrics to the beat. Create any two sets of rhyming words, sing the first one twice, then the second once, for your own blues verse!

Track 5: The Boogie Woogie Breathing Pattern

"Boogie Woogie" or "Barrelhouse Blues" music was born perhaps a century ago, where the Mississippi River runs into the Gulf of Mexico. These often lively and upbeat "Delta" Blues styles came up the river before WW II, and developed into the electrically-amplified Chicago Blues group styles. The Muddy Waters Band, with harpist "Little Walter," was one of the greatest of these.

Chicago Blues Master

Marion "Little Walter" Jacobs R.I.P.

Don Mayne

A great deal of classic and modern rock music uses the Boogie Woogie as a foundation. And as you may know, *most* modern American music — rock, jazz, soul, R n' B, and rap — owes a tremendous debt to those early African-American originators of the Blues. Anyone who loves music must pay homage to these original masters, who gave the world many of its greatest forms of artistic self-expression, with so little recognition or reward!

The Boogie Woogie Breathing Pattern

Listen a few times before trying it on the 4, 5, and 6 hole, then make the changes fast and crisp. Repeat this two bar (eight beat) Breathing Pattern until it feels familiar!

in   out   in   out   in   out   in   (two silent beats)

456   456   **456**   456   **456**   456   **456**

The last "out-in" part is tricky for some, so I'll describe it in more detail on the next page.

The Boogie Woogie Beat

Notice that the last *"out-in"* is squashed into a single beat.

in out **in** out **in** out **in** (two silent beats)
one beat

If this confuses you, listen to my foot taps on the CD. The last out breath happens just as my foot hits the floor. The last in breath happens as my foot comes back up, but ends just before my foot taps again (which is the first of the two silent beats). I show this visually by having a dot over the out breath, and no dot over the in.

Movin' It Around

Just like we did with the Chicago Breathing Pattern, we'll practice using the Boogie Woogie Breathing Pattern on holes 6, 7, and 8, and then on holes 8, 9, and 10.

one beat

678 678 **678** 678 **678** 678 **678**

I won't write the 8, 9, and 10 hole version out in notation — it looks harder than it is (too many numbers). Just aim your mouth at the highest holes, and play the Breathing Pattern.

> Some Blues or rock riffs or solos look scary in notation but are easy to play. So I may just write out in words what you need to do. Often, it won't matter much *exactly* which holes you play, as long as the Breathing Pattern is right...

Two Boogie Woogie Blues Verses

Now you're ready to play along with my blues band — bass, drums, and rhythm guitar. Aim your mouth at holes 4, 5, and 6, and get ready for the first in breath at the count of four!

Your First Boogie Woogie Verse

In the first verse, just repeat the Boogie Woogie Breathing Pattern six times on the 4, 5, and 6 holes.

Just repeat the following line six times (6 two bar riffs = 12 Bars)

456 456 **456** 456 **456** 456 **456** (two silent beats)

Remember to stay *empty* enough during the two beats of silence so that you can start the next riff on an in breath.

Your Second Boogie Woogie Verse

I'll talk you through it, using the Boogie Woogie Breathing Pattern to play riffs on the 4, 5, and 6 holes, the 6, 7, and 8 holes, and the 8, 9, and 10 holes. You'll combine these three riffs to play a more exciting Boogie Woogie Twelve Bar Blues Verse!

> **Note:** This *looks* way harder than it is to *play!*

(Starts at 4:08 of Track 5.)

456 456 **456** 456 **456** 456 **456**

456 456 **456** 456 **456** 456 **456**

678 678 **678** 678 **678** 678 **678**

456 456 **456** 456 **456** 456 **456**

8910 8910 **8910** 8910 **8910** 8910 **8910**

456 456 **456** 456 **456** 456 **456**

Great Playalong Hint

Does your sound system have a stereo balance control? In many of the recorded exercises that have background music, you can get rid of either my voice (usually on the right), my harmonica (usually on the left), or sometimes both, by using the left/right balance control.

About "Track Times"

Every so often (like on the previous page), you'll see a small note that looks like this:

(Starts at 4:08 of Track 5)

(4:08 of Track 5)   Or you may see even simpler ones, that look like these at left and right.   (4:08)

These are "Track Times" to help you locate an exercise, riff, or verse within the longer CD tracks. Most CD players will show you how long a track has been playing. For example, when you are playing Track 5, seeing a readout of 4:08 means that you have played 4 minutes and 8 seconds of Track 5. These notes may be useful if you want to play a short section over and over, without either listening to the entire track or having to search the whole track for a particular spot.

Getting Ready for Songs and the Song Sections

Are you more interested in playing songs or melodies — that is, the tune of a well-known song — than in playing Blues or rock music? If so, you'll like the next track. And now, a special hint for song lovers:

Make sure that you look at the written notation while you play *Taps*, even if you can play it from the instructions on the CD, or by ear. Why? Because you may need to use the notation in "The Song Sections" — which contain additional melodies — to play more complex tunes.

Track 6: Your First Folk Song

In this track you won't just learn how to play your first folk song. You'll also find that you don't have to be a highly experienced harmonica player to express emotion through your instrument. In addition, you'll begin to learn to navigate your way around the harmonica, hole by hole. This will help you to play more interesting folk, Blues, and rock songs.

Navigation: The Hole Thing

Follow the instructions on the recording, and practice locating the holes 3, 4, 5, and 6. This does not — repeat not — mean that I want you to play them as single notes. It merely means that I want you to be able to *aim* your lips at the center of each hole (while covering the holes on either side) with some degree of confidence.

Aim, don't obsess!
Start Full —   3   4   5   6
all OUT notes!

Practice, take your time, and don't be self-critical. As I said, the same hand/mouth coordination that allows you to safely feed yourself with a pointy fork will help you to do this, with just a bit of work.

Taps: Lots of Emotion, Not Much Technique

This lovely campfire song is traditionally used to express a range of wistful or sad emotion, from noting the end of a great day outdoors as you sit around the embers of the campfire, to mourning a fallen comrade. It's easy to play, using just four notes, all on the out breath — but play it with feeling. It's never too soon to start expressing your feelings through the harmonica. Simple as it is, it's one of my favorite, and emotionally satisfying, songs...

From now on, I'll usually write out a song using single notes instead of chords — mainly to save space, and because it looks less cluttered.

You'll still use the *"aim technique."* Just aim your mouth at the single hole I write down, but keep it slightly open, to include the holes on each side. This'll give you the right chords to play the song.

Songs often sound better when played with chords, or a combination of single holes and chords, than if played with single holes only.

Taps

(Starts at 1:55)

Taps starts at the count of three, not four, so listen to me play it, then join me. Start with your lungs fairly full, and catch a quick breath whenever you need to (the silent beats provide you with lots of time to do this). Notice that many of the notes occur *in between* the beats — while your foot is up in the air. These are the notes that do not have a dot over them.

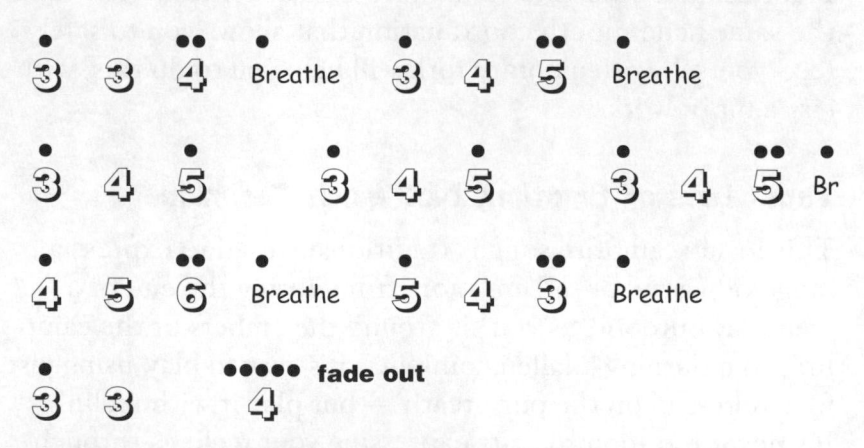

Catch a quick breath during the silent beats. But make sure that you don't accidentally play an "in" sound on the harmonica when you do — the next page will help you to avoid that!

Catching Your Breath, and Wooziness

You'll often need to catch a quick in or out breath when playing. Obviously, if your lungs are getting too full, you'll have to let some air out. And if you're getting too empty, you'll have to get some air in. Most songs or riffs have silent beats that you can catch a breath during. Sometimes you'll even have to catch a quick one between notes.

The easiest way to catch a quick breath is this:

Keep your upper lip on the harmonica. Drop your lower lip about 1/4 inch, and grab the breath from *under* the harmonica! This won't make an unwanted sound, and it won't take your mouth away from the hole that you're on! And if you ever feel woozy while playing, read on.

No matter what shape you are in, playing harmonica is likely to make you use more air than you're used to. This can produce a little bit of wooziness. If it does, just take a break for a minute. After a week or so, you'll have to play really hard to get woozy. I like to play as I run (and have a whole program on "Harmonica-robic™" conditioning). Sometimes I even get a bit spacey, especially if I'm going fast on an uphill!

Improvisation Versus Note-for-Note Playing

In Blues and rock, there's room to be creative with the notes you use — that's just improvisation, or making up your own riffs as you play! But when playing folk or classical songs (especially songs that listeners may know), it's important to aim in the right vicinity, and to keep track of the ins and outs.

What's Next?

Go on to Tracks 7 and 8 for some technique. Then Tracks 9 through 12 for more Blues and rock, or Track 13 for more songs.

Track 7: More on Beat, Rhythm, and Breathing Patterns

I would like to mention that a good sense of rhythm is not something that most of us are born with. Rather, it can be learned. Please don't be embarrassed to do some of the things I suggest in this track — I do 'em on a daily basis, to keep my sense of rhythm in good shape!

Obviously, developing a good sense of rhythm is one of those things that's better learned by listening and doing than by reading about. So if you have trouble tapping your foot in time with me, or if you can't seem to maintain the Breathing Patterns, this track (of the CD) will help more than anything I write here.

If you've had trouble with the Breathing Patterns in Track 2, it will be worth your while to read all of this track. Otherwise, just skim it.

Bars and Measures

Blues, rock, and other types of musicians often break a rhythm pattern into chunks of four beats each, called *"bars"* or *"measures."* Count some bars along with me, and count some next time you are walking, too. Say each number — from one to four — at the exact instant your foot hits the floor!

One   Two   Three   Four

Breathing Pattern Review

Have you had problems with the Breathing Patterns? If you have, I've provided extra help in the recording for this track. The following written hints and details may also help.

The Ins and Outs of Breathing

Since we're used to talking on the out breath only, we're very used to paying attention to the use of the out breath. We just grab a quick inhale as needed, so that we can talk some more.

As we always talk on the out breath, we usually start all of our sentences by taking an in breath beforehand. But many of the Breathing Patterns start on an in breath, so we need to be at least somewhat (or sometimes very) empty as we begin.

So harp players must develop control of our in breaths as well as our outs. We have to control both the inhale and exhales — we can't just breathe in or out as we please anymore!

Practice some "in - out - in" breaths without the harmonica. Pay close attention to how it feels, in your lungs, your mouth, your stomach muscles. Intense focus on the breath is great for stress reduction, as you'll learn when you get to Track 21!

Close the Nose, Open the Mind

Try not to lose air through your nose as you play — that's as big a waste as self-critical thoughts when you hit a bum note during a song! I'll give you more instruction on nose closing in the next track.

Now, if you need Breathing Pattern practice, work along with my detailed instructions for this "in-out-in-beat" Breathing Pattern on the recording.

456   **456**   **456**   (silent beat)

> **Remember: Outlined Means Breathe OUT!**
> **And when in doubt, listen to the recording!**

Now go back to Track Three if you came here from Track Two to get extra help, or else continue on to Track Eight.

Track 8: Harmonica Tone and Special Effects

As I wrote at the beginning of Track Seven, some things are better heard than read. Harmonica tone effects are among them. But that doesn't mean that harmonica tone is not important, and there are years of work in this track — I still work on my tone and special effects every day! By the way: the music you hear as I introduce this track is based on the "Dirty Dirty Dog" pattern described later on in this track, combined with "dwah" effects (described in Track 15) and a few advanced "bending" techniques (touched upon later).

Wide Open Spaces

The more open space there is in your mouth and throat, the better tone you'll have. To make open space in the mouth, keep your tongue relaxed and low in the mouth as you play, and your teeth at least slightly apart. See page 39 for more on this...

Keeping open space in your throat, which I define as going down as far as the stomach, is harder, but can offer great benefits.

Deeper Breathing

Try to breathe from your stomach. What does that mean? Well, many of us tend to breathe shallowly, using mostly the muscles of our chest rather than the dinner-plate shaped diaphragm muscle that separates our lungs from our other internal organs. When we breathe in, the diaphragm flexes downward, pulling air down into our lungs. When we breathe out, it flexes upwards, pushing the air up and out.

Stomach Breathing Exercise

Here's an exercise that will help you to focus your attention on breathing from the stomach. Stand in a relaxed position, both hands on your stomach. As you breathe in, gently expand your belly — you'll be able to feel it bulging out with your hands. As you breathe out, contract your stomach muscles, so that your stomach becomes flatter. (I don't say flat because mine never is, anymore!) If this feels un-natural — the opposite of how you usually breathe — you're probably a "chest-breather," and fill your chest first, *then* your stomach.

By gently practicing this exercise, you'll improve both your breathing and your tone! Harmonica playing can really help your respiration — if this interests you, see the "Where To Go from Here" section on my book *Better Breathing Through Harmonica,* used by rehab facilities in various parts of the nation!

Close the Nose!

Most of us never consciously use the muscles of our soft palate (at the back of the throat) to close the nasal passage and separate our nose from our mouth.

So just think of blowing out birthday candles to keep your nose shut on the out breaths. Think of drinking a thickshake through a straw to keep your nose shut while inhaling. Feel those throat muscles tighten!

Attack that Harp! (Demonstrated on Track 8 at :38)

Soft and hard, flowing and sharp, sliding gently from place to place or starting each sound with an aggressive puff of air — there are many different ways to play even a single chord.

> This is all on the recording, so listen and you'll begin to develop your own style of "harp attack."

Articulation (Track 8 at 1:15)

Articulation is nothing more than a fancy name for *whispering* words like "duh" or "tuh" through the harmonica. Whispering (not *saying*) multiple "duh duh duh duh" sequences is an easy way to break a note or chord into lots of short, sharp, pieces.

It's much easier to do all of these articulations on the out breaths. But if you start empty and simply make your tongue and lips go through the same whispering motions, you'll get the in-articulations. Took me years of practice, to do it really well.

The Dirty Dirty Dogs: Classical Versus Swing!

The four beat "Dirty Dirty Dog • " is one of my very favorite articulations, as described in detail on the recording. Here are the "Non-Swinging" Dirty Dogs (as a classical musician would say them, if classical musicians did, which they don't).

One Bar Non-Swinging Dogs: European Musical Tradition
(Each divided beat broken into two equal parts)

•   •   •
Dir   tee   Dir   tee   Dog   (silent)

It's much more fun if you "swing" the Dirty Dog rhythm. The bold syllables are emphasized, as you'll hear on the recording.

One Bar Swinging Dogs: African-American Musical Tradition
(The "downbeat" part of a divided beat held longer than the "upbeat")

•   •   •   •
Dirrr   d'   Dirrr   d'   Dog   (silent)

Whisper (don't say) it through the middle of the harmonica. If I want you to use a specific articulation, I'll write it down. In swing beats, I'll make the upbeats (shorter parts) smaller.

dirrr   d'   dirrr   d'   dog
•   •   •
456   456   **456**   456   **456**   (silent)

Puttin' Out the Dogs   (Track 8 at 2:35)

Start on the out breath, and whisper some Dirty Dirty Dogs forcefully in different places on the harp: low, middle, high.

Then lick your lips and move or slide the harmonica during a few bars of exhaled Dirty Dirty Dogs. Start low and end high, or start high and end low, or move around during this articulation in any way you can think of.   Don't worry about playing each riff exactly as I do. Just start in the middle, head up toward the high holes, then work your way down.

| • • • • |
| Each "Dirty Dirty Dog Beat" riff is one bar (4 beats) long. |

dirrr	d'	dirrr	d'	dog	
•		•		•	•
456	456	**567**	567	**678**	(silent)

dirrr	d'	dirrr	d'	dog	
•		•		•	•
789	789	**567**	567	**456**	(silent)

Doggin' It In

Unfortunately, you also need to do the Dirty Dogs on the in breaths. Start empty, keep your nose shut, and just start doing it, odd as it may feel. Once you can do an in Dirty Dirty Dog in one place, lick your lips and move it around!

dirrr	d'	dirrr	d'	dog	
•		•		•	•
456	456	**567**	567	**678**	(silent)

dirrr	d'	dirrr	d'	dog	
•		•		•	•
789	789	**567**	567	**456**	(silent)

But don't get hung up here — spend a minute on the in Dogs, then come back to them later (for the next few weeks). In the meantime, go on to Track 9, in both book and recording.

Track 9: Slidin', Shakin', Doggin', and some Crucial Advice

As I say in the intro to this track, *perfecting* the material in Technique Tracks Seven, Eight, and Nine could easily take years of work. The music behind my voice consists mostly of alternating in and out Dirty Dogs, with slides and shakes added, and ending (recognize it?) with a shakin' Chicago riff.

Sliding and Shaking

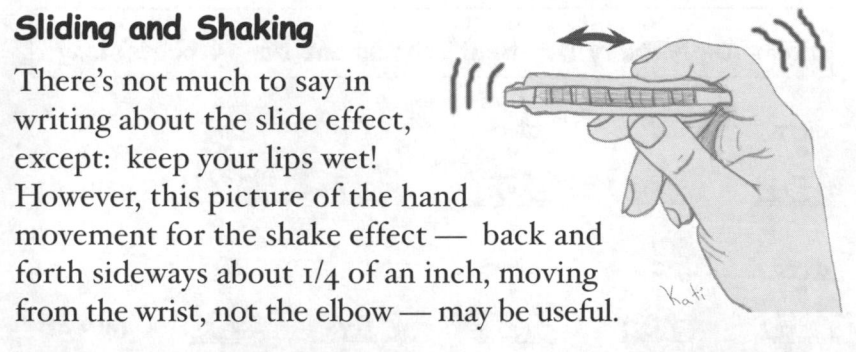

There's not much to say in writing about the slide effect, except: keep your lips wet! However, this picture of the hand movement for the shake effect — back and forth sideways about 1/4 of an inch, moving from the wrist, not the elbow — may be useful.

The shake will feel awkward at first, but it gets easier as the neurons of your brain memorize the hand movement. Soon it'll be as easy as brushing your teeth! Apply the shake to the Chicago and Boogie Woogie Breathing Patterns, as in my recorded examples, to create some great riffs!

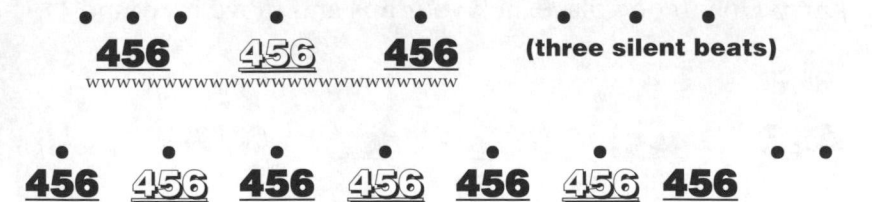

I put a wavy line under chords that I want you to shake on.

When you can add a "bending" effect to a shake — as I do while talking about "...a good shake takes a long time to develop" — you'll be playing pro-level harp (at least for a riff or two)!

Dirty Dog Effects

Now it's time to combine some of the special effects with the Dirty Dirty Dog articulation. Practice shaking some dogs, alternating a bar of in Dirty Dogs with a bar of out Dirty Dogs, as in my recorded example using only the middle holes.

Try playing the Dirty Dirty in the middle, and the Dog a hole or two higher, or a hole or two lower. Here's the example I used for this, with a shake on the second and third beat of the in part, followed of course by the silent beat:

Dirr	d'	Dirr	d'	Dog		
•		•		•	•	Bar of
345	**345**	**345**	**345**	**456**		In Dogs!

wwwwwwwwwwwwwwwwwww

Dirr	d'	Dirr	d'	Dog		
				•	•	Bar of
345	345	345	345	234		Out Dogs!

Movin' the Dirty Dog Riffs

You can move during your entire Dirty Dirty Dog too, as I do in my example, going up on the ins, then back down on the outs. Don't try to play just what I do — instead, make up any variation you like on this!

Dirr	d'	Dirr	d'	Dog		
•		•		•	•	Bar of
345	**345**	**456**	**456**	**789**		In Dogs!

Dirr	d'	Dirr	d'	Dog		
				•	•	Bar of
567	567	345	345	234		Out Dogs!

Practice playing one set (4 beats, one bar) of In Dogs, then playing one set (4 beats, one bar) of Out Dogs. This forms a very cool two bar riff that you'll have some fun with soon!

Slidin' the Dirty Dog Riffs — Mine and Yours

Slide those Dogs, too! Try a low to high slide for each dirr, back down on the d' — or start with slide on the first dirr, and work your way down slowly. Once again, these are just suggestions to help you create your own riffs. I won't write them down, as I *don't* want you to dutifully memorize and repeat my riffs (unless you want to). I'd rather you make up your own!

The Dirty Dog Two Chord Rock Jamm   (Begins at 2:10)

After you've done your Dog practice, apply what you've learned by playing them along with a popular style of classic rock and roll, which I call *"Two Bar Two Chord Rock."* Some of my favorite classic rock musicians, from Donovan to J. Geils, use this particular chord structure or chord progression.

In this style of music the guitar and bass player alternate playing two chords, for one bar each, so the pattern repeats itself every two bars. One chord (the "G chord") fits in very well with thc *inhaled* Dirty Dogs. The other chord (the "C chord") fits in very well with the *exhaled* Dirty Dogs.

So play along with me: one set of Dogs on the in breath (don't forget the silent beat!), then one set of Dogs on the out: back and forth, in then out, along with my rock and roll band.

There are many other riffs that can be played along with this type of rock music (and I'll throw in a few "non-Dog" riffs at the end). But for now stick with the Dirty Dogs, alternating one bar of in Dogs with one bar of out Dogs. However, I mostly want you to practice the Dogs as a rhythm exercise — we'll use this Dog rhythm in a more interesting way in Track 20.

If you like this style of music, come back to it and play along. Remember: if you have a stereo system with a left/right control, you can lose my voice and harmonica. Oh — and the verbal advice I offer towards the end of this track is, in my humble opinion, the most important part of this method...

Track 10: Rockin' The Blues

In the last track, you practiced moving around during your Dirty Dirty Dogs. Now it's time to practice moving around, shaking, and sliding as we play the Boogie Woogie Breathing Pattern. After that, we'll use it in a very entertaining way!

Shakin' and Movin' the Boogie Woogie

You have already, I hope, practiced using your shake *during* a Boogie Woogie Breathing Pattern. Now it's time to add some movement, too. So lick your lips and move while you play this great Breathing Pattern, which I'll write down right here for your convenience.

in out in out in out in (silent beats)

Try playing one that's similar to my example. I start in the middle, and work my way up at the high end, making sure to follow the breathing pattern. Then, after the two silent beats, I begin the next Boogie Woogie Breathing Pattern at the high end, and work my way down, in and out, to finish it off in the middle. I won't write these out — I'd rather that you create your own variations.

Improvise! Create Your Own Riffs, Along with Me!

Once you learn to move around during a Breathing Pattern, you are improvising — creating your own music as you play! No longer are you playing riffs of mine. Instead, you're coming up with riffs of your own, since only you can choose where and how and when to move. Although I love to play riffs composed by the master players, and love to play songs of all types, there is no more creative and free way of making music than improvisation! In just a moment, we'll improvise some Boogie Woogie Breathing Pattern riffs, together!

A Heavy "Rock Boogie" (Begins at :40)

Now it's time for a duet. Alternate some Boogie Woogie
Breathing Patterns with me — I'll play one, then you! We'll
use a dramatic *"Rock Boogie"* rhythm for background music.

A Boogie is a particular blues/rock rhythm with a heavy,
almost menacing sound. Bands like Canned Heat, Z.Z. Top,
and the great, late, Bluesman John Lee Hooker often play(ed)
Boogies that use just one chord. Booker T's "Green Onions"
and Sonny Boy Williamson's "Help Me" are examples of
Boogies that use three chords. Regardless of the number of
chords used, the Rock Boogie rhythm and the Boogie Woogie
Breathing Pattern go together like ribs and hot sauce!

My verbal instructions will help you, if you need it. If you
like, try to play what I do. Or try to play something similar
— perhaps with the same effects, but a different movement
of the harmonica. Or just get ideas from listening to my riffs,
and improvise — see what comes out!

If you like this Rock Boogie style, you've got a treat coming
in Track 20. Use your stereo control to lose my voice or harp.

By the Way: Try a Two Hole Chord

Now might be a good time to start playing some chords using
just two holes. To do this, you'll have to aim your mouth a bit
differently. Use your tongue to identify the divider between
holes 4 and 5. Then aim your mouth at that divider, while
puckering your lips out just a little. This will make the opening
of your mouth a slightly smaller, so if you aim at the 4/5
divider, you'll cover just the 4 and the 5 holes.

Once you get the hang of it, play some two hole Boogie
Woogie Breathing Pattern riffs. A two hole shake sounds
crisper than a three hole shake. Start by aiming at the divider
between holes 4 and 5, and try to shake only far enough to
center on 4, then on 5, as your hand moves.

Track 11: Movin' to Chicago

We did it with the Dirty Dogs. We did it with the Boogie Woogie. Now it's time to start moving *during* the Chicago Breathing Pattern. My favorite way to do this is to move only once, just before the last in breath.

The Main Chicago Riff

Here's my favorite example, which I call the "Main" Chicago riff (my name for it, not everyone's). I usually shake it during the long in breath, but you could shake the entire riff, as well. (Try it using two note chords on 45 in, 45 out, and 34, also.)

456 456 **345** (three silent beats)
wwwwww

Of course, you can start this riff anywhere you like (as you remember — that's the beauty of Breathing Patterns). Try aiming at the 6 hole, to start it. Throw in a shake, for fun.

567 567 **456**
wwwwww

Ending a Verse with Class: The Chicago "Turnaround"

A *"turnaround"* is a musical announcement that one blues verse is ending, and another about to begin. One easy and commonly used turnaround involves nothing more complex than an inhaled slide downward, ending on the 1 in note.

234 234 slide **1**
wwwwww

If I want you to slide between two notes, I'll write "slide" (tricky, eh?). If the word "slide" is outlined, you breathe out during the slide. If "slide" is filled in, breathe in during it. We mostly use in slides, often coming — fast — after an out chord.

An Easy Single Note: the 1 In

It's relatively easy to get a single note on the lowest hole. All you have to do is angle the harmonica so that the high end is away from your face. This pushes the low end of the harmonica deep into your mouth — don't be afraid to let the low end corner go right in!

A Dynamite 16 Beat Breathing Pattern (Track 11 at 1:10)

Combining the two bar Boogie Woogie Breathing Pattern with the two bar Chicago Breathing Pattern provides us with a great four bar Breathing Pattern that can be used to improvise along with either Blues and rock music. You've done each one separately — now just put them together, like this:

in out in out in out in

innnnn   out   in   (three silent beats)

Practice the new breathing pattern a few times without moving, in the middle. Then try my first example (which begins at 1:15):

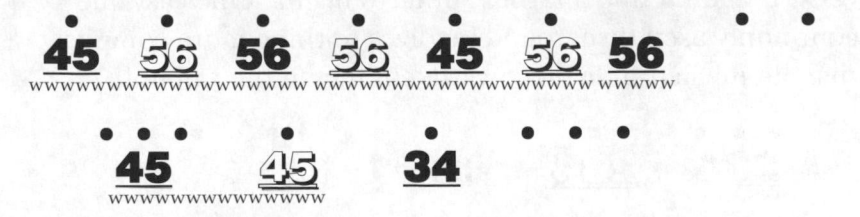

45 56 56 56 45 56 56
wwwwwwwwwwwwwwww wwwwwwwwwwwwwwwww wwwww

45   45   34
wwwwwwwwwwwww

On the recording, I'll help you, breath by breath, to use this four bar Breathing Pattern along with my band. Playing three of these four bar patterns will produce (since 3 times 4 bars always equals twelve bars) — one fine Twelve Bar Blues verse.

The Boogie Woogie Chicago Blues Verse

Listen to me play the verse a few times before you try it, so you'll be prepared for the ways in which I ask you to move the Breathing Patterns around. You'll use your new Chicago Turnaround, from page 35, to end the solo (it's the last line).

As usual, the notation look harders than it plays. So if you're a "listen learner," forget this page! But either way, try to use two note chords, if you can.

(Begins at 1:45)

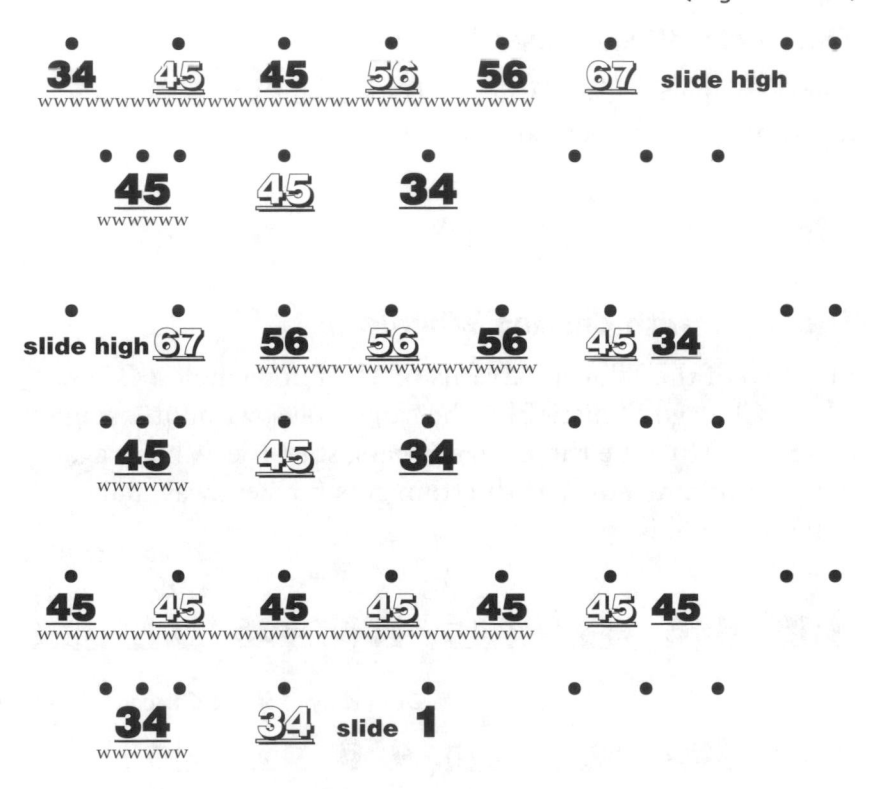

It Works Great Anywhere!

Also, at the end of this track, I'll give you a short example to demonstrate how well this four bar Breathing Pattern fits into the Rock Boogie from Track 10, so feel free to go to the Rock Boogie Playalong Track 24 or the Guitar Blues Playalong Track 22, and have some fun right now!

Track 12: The Rockin' Blues Train

Sometimes you just don't feel like bringing your own rock band along with you on the camping trip. Perhaps you don't even have a boombox in your backpack. That's when the train comes in handy! It's easy to play, and it sounds great without any other background music but the steady beat of your feet as you hike down the trail.

The Train Wheels Breathing Pattern

Here's the basic "Train Wheels" Breathing Pattern. Try it a few times *without* your harmonica.

• • • • • • • •
in **in** out out **in** **in** out out

The Train with Chicago Whistle

Play two of the Wheel Patterns on the middle holes. Then add a "Chicago Whistle" on the same holes, without losing the beat. After the three silent beats, start the Wheels again, fade the volume down as the train gets further away, and that's all there is to it!

(Begins at 1:10)

• • • • • • • •
456 **456** 456 456 **456** **456** 456 456

"Get ready for the Chicago whistle"
• • • • • • • •
456 **456** 456 456 **456** **456** 456 456

••• • •
456 456 **456** "Back to the double in"
wwwwwwwwwwww

• • • • • • • •
456 **456** 456 456 **456** **456** 456 456

The Low Down Train, and the Terrible Twos!

The train sounds better if you play the Wheel Pattern using the 1, 2, and 3 holes of the harmonica, as written for you on the next page. Unfortunately, it's hard for beginning players to get a good tone out of the low end of the "C" harmonica...

"My Harmonica is Broken"

I wish I had a nickel for every workshop student who has come up and said, "My 2 in note is broken!" In 99.9% of the cases, the harmonica is not the problem.

Low End Corner of
Harmonica inside cheek

The 2 in note of the "C" harp is hard to play. That's just the way it is, on every "C" harp. If the harp's not far enough into your mouth — you get a "choked" or "funky" sound on the 123 in chord.

The low end corner of the harmonica should be tucked inside your cheek. Here's a test: if the harmonica won't stay in your mouth with "no hands," it's not in far enough for a beginner to get a good low in chord. (But don't *play* with no hands — that's just to test if it's in deep enough!)

Sweet and Low: Good Tone on the Low In Chord

The CD will help you on the 123 in chord. With harmonica deep in mouth and mouth as relaxed and open as possible, start on the 123 out chord, then change ever so slowly and gently to the 123 in chord. If you absolutely can't get a good tone on it, keep your nose open, just this once. Keep your tongue relaxed, and a "soft attack" (no articulation, low volume). Once you have a non-choked sound, slowly start playing the out-in chords faster and more crisply. You won't need to keep the harmonica so far into your mouth anymore, either, once you get the hang of it.

That Low Down Train

Once you've practiced getting good low end tone, and can play a low Wheels Pattern without funky tone — play a low end train with the Main Chicago Riff Whistle. It's a real crowd pleaser, especially when kids are in the crowd! Here's my recorded example, played just before I began talking about the troubles with 2 in...

(Demonstrated at 1:50)

•   •   •   •   •   •   •   •
123 **123** 123 123 **123** **123** 123 123

•   •   •   •   •   •   •   •
123 **123** 123 123 **123** **123** 123 123

•••   •   •   •••
45 **45** **34**
wwwwwwwwwwww

"Chukka" That Train!

Now that you can (I hope, most of the time) get a decent tone out of the 123 in chord, you're ready to add a "chukka chukka" articulation on the two out breaths of the Wheels Pattern. This makes your train sound, well, trainier. Just whisper one chukka through each of those two out breaths: "in-in-chukka-chukka." Some people find it easier to do at first *without* the harmonica — although you may want to practice *that* in private!

(Begins at 3:30)

          chukka chukka   chukka chukka
•   •   •   •   •   •   •   •
123 **123** 123 123 **123** **123** 123 123

          chukka chukka   chukka chukka
•   •   •   •   •   •   •   •
123 **123** 123 123 **123** **123** 123 123

Throw in Some Train Whistles

You've already used the Chicago riff with your train. Now add a Boogie Woogie Breathing Pattern, or even a four bar Boogie Woogie plus Chicago Breathing pattern.

Just come back to the basic Wheel Pattern every so often, and you'll have an exciting balance between wild soloing and a solid rhythm section — all provided by you!

A Train Wheel Hint

When playing the train, as any good engineer would, keep a close eye on the fuel (your breath). If you start feeling too empty, either soften your out breaths or strengthen your ins. Too full? Do the reverse — softer ins, or harder outs. After some practice, you won't even have to think about it.

A Whistle Hint: Silences are Golden

Use the beats of silence at the end of the Chicago and Boogie Woogie Breathing Patterns to catch your breath if need be, and find your way back to the low in chord that begins the next Wheel Pattern. Don't forget them, and lose your rhythm!

A Train in the Brain

Once you feel comfortable with these Breathing Patterns, improvise with the Breathing Patterns to make the train your own. As all actions in the world originate on the level of thought, imagine your train as you play it.

Are you on the train? Then the sound level stays the same, although the speed may vary as it slows down or speeds up. Is it coming towards you as you wait at the station? It'll get louder and slower, until it stops! Leaving you behind at the depot? It'll speed up, and get softer, until it's so far away that you can no longer hear the clacking of the wheels — only a faint whistle, wafting back to you on the wind...

Track 13: Folk Songs & the Major Scale

In this track, you'll begin learning one of the two *"Musical Alphabets"* that provide the building blocks for much of the Western World's music. But first, a bit of navigation review.

From Four to Six

Practice locating the holes 4, 5, and 6, with an out breath on each. Use the very tip of your tongue to locate and count each hole up from the low end, to get a feel for the distance between them. Just aim — forget single notes.

● ● ● ● ● ● ● ●
4 5 6   4 5 6   **All Outs!**

For a real-world review, go back to page 22 and give me a round of *Taps!*

The Major Scale: A Musical Alphabet

The 26 letters of the English alphabet are used in various combinations to create words, sentences, paragraphs, and libraries full of books. The letters of the Russian alphabet produce Russian words, and long, sad Russian novels.

"Scales" are musical alphabets — their notes are used as the building blocks for riffs and songs and solos. You'll learn two scales in this method. The first one is called the *"Major Scale."* It's used to play thousands of songs.

If you want to play folk or classical music, make sure to practice the first six notes of this scale, right now. Of course, you'll be playing these as chords now, not single holes or notes, since we haven't gotten around to them yet!

Playing the Major Scale, Do to La

Here are the first six notes of the easiest Major Scale on the harmonica (you'll find the remaining two notes in Track 18, but you can play lots of songs with just this much). I'll write this scale out in single notes. You may be familiar with these notes by their names "do-re-mi-fa-so-la."

4	4	5	5	6	6
DO	RE	ME	FA	SO	LA

Now I'll write the same thing out as chords, since that's how I expect you to be playing it for now.

(Track 13 at 1:10)

345 **345** **456** **456** **567** **567**

> Practice this Major Scale a few times right now!

Twinkle Twinkle, Piece by Piece

Spend a moment on the 4 to 6 jump. You'll actually be jumping from the 3, 4, and 5 out chord to the 5, 6, and 7 out chord. Once you've practiced this, you're ready for the first part of the song. Childish? Maybe. But a great scale exercise!

Twinkle Twinkle Little Star is composed of only three parts, each eight beats long. Here's the first, written out as single notes (but play them as chords). Practice each part along with my verbal instructions on the recording.

(2:05)

Twin	kle	twin	kle	lit	tle	star	(breath)
•	•	•	•	•	•	•	•
4	4	6	6	6	6	6	

Now try the second part.

(2:30)

How	I	won	der	what	you	are	
•	•	•	•	•	•	••	
5	5	5	5	4	4	4	(quick breath)

Practice with the CD (at 2:50) and put the two parts together!

Twin	kle	twin	kle	lit	tle	star	(breath)
•	•	•	•	•	•	•	•
4	4	6	6	**6**	**6**	6	

How	I	won	der	what	you	are	
•	•	•	•	•	•	••	
5	**5**	5	5	**4**	**4**	4	(quick breath)

Now learn the last part. In the actual song (below), you'll play it twice in the second line. So be ready to make the jump from the 4 in of the word "high" to the 6 out of the word "Like."

(3:35)

Up	a	bove	the	world	so	high	(breath)
•	•	•	•	•	•	•	•
6	6	**5**	**5**	5	5	**4**	

Twinkle Twinkle Little Star

Now you're ready to play the whole thing! Just listen to me playing and giving vocal instructions before you try it, and don't be self-critical. As I say in my corporate psychology harmonica workshops: "Any attention paid to self-critical or negative thoughts during a task is wasted energy, as big a waste as letting air escape through your nose when you play!"

(4:25)

Twin	kle	twin	kle	lit	tle	star			How	I	won	der	what	you	are
•	•	•	•	•	•	•	•		•	•	•	•	•	•	•
4	4	6	6	**6**	**6**	6			**5**	**5**	5	5	**4**	**4**	4

Up	a	bove	the	world	so	high			Like	a	dia	mond	in	the	sky	
•	•	•	•	•	•	•	•		•	•	•	•	•	•	•	•
6	6	**5**	**5**	5	5	**4**			6	6	**5**	**5**	5	5	**4**	

Twin	kle	twin	kle	lit	tle	star			How	I	won	der	what	you	are
•	•	•	•	•	•	•	•		•	•	•	•	•	•	••
4	4	6	6	**6**	**6**	6			**5**	**5**	5	5	**4**	**4**	4

Amazing Grace

This beautiful song can be broken down into three parts as simply as *Twinkle Twinkle Little Star.* Practice each separately, then put them together. Listen to me on the recording first: I'll talk you through each part, note by note, breath by breath.

Amazing Grace Part One (6:00)   **Amazing Grace Part Two** (6:35)

A	maz	ing	grace		How	sweet	the	sound
•	••	•	••		•	••	•	••
3	4	5	5		**4**	**4**	**6**	6

Amazing Grace Part Three (8:00)

I	once	was	lost
•	••	•	••
5	6	4	5

Put these three parts together with a few slight variations, and you've got the entire song.

Look at the entire song, below. You've already learned the first line. The second line is almost the same as the first — just add a 4 in to 6 out to Part One. The third line combines Part Three with Part Two. And the last line begins with Part One, adds a 4 in to 4 out, then slides up on the out notes. In the version below, I offer a few extra places to catch a breath.

(Whole song begins 9:20)

A	maz	ing	grace		How	sweet	the	sound		(breath)
•	••	•	••		•	••	•	•		•
3	4	5	5		**4**	**4**	**6**	6		

To	save	a	wretch		like	me		(breath)
•	••	•	••		•	•••		••
3	4	5	5		**4**	6		

I	once	was	lost		but	now	am	found		(breath)
•	••	•	••		•	••	•	•		•
5	6	4	5		**4**	**4**	**6**	6		

Was	blind	but	now		can	see			
•	••	•	••		•	•	•	•	••
3	4	5	5		**4**	**4**	5	6	7

Track 14: Harder Songs & Minor Music

Now it's time to play a song that you probably know very well since childhood, but which has a more complex rhythm.

My Country 'tis of Thee

My	coun	try	'tis	of	thee		sweet	land	of	lib	er	ty
•	•	•	••		•		•	•	•	••		•
4	4	**4**	**3**	4	4		5	5	5	5	**4**	4

of	thee	I	sing	•
•	•	•	•••	
4	4	**3**	4	

Land	where	my	fa	thers	died		Land	of	the	Pil	grim's	pride
•	•	•	••	•	•		•	•	•	•	•	•
6	6	6	6	**5**	5		**5**	**5**	**5**	**5**	5	**6**

From	e	ev	e	ry	moun	tain	side	le	et	free	dom	ring
•	•	•	•	•	••		•	•	•	•	•	••••
5	**5**	5	**4**	4	**5**	**5**	**6**	6	**6**	5	**4**	4

> If that was not too hard, you are now ready to go to The Song Section on page 74 and play any of the Major Scale songs.

The Minor Scale

The *"Minor Scale"* is the second of the two musical alphabets that are used to play a great deal of our so-called Western Civilization's music. It tends to have a more plaintive or eerie sound than the more upbeat sounding Major Scale.

4	5	**5**	6	**6**	7	7	**8**
D	E	F	G	A	B	C	D

Although I've written it out in single hole notation, you can aim your slightly opened mouth at the hole number I've written, and let the neighboring hole on each side play. But...

Single Notes or Chords?   Learn It Now or Later?

But the Minor Scale is a bit less forgiving than the Major, so it may be worth using the single note advice on page 52, then coming back and playing the Minor Scale again.

If you like, you can begin practicing the Minor Scale now, although it will be the hardest thing you've tried so far. Once you can play it from left to right (low to high), try it right to left (high to low). This, by the way, is a "Dorian" Minor Scale.

Or perhaps you'd prefer to learn the Minor Scale by playing a song or two first — that's all right by me (and may be easier)!

What Shall We Do With a Drunken Sailor?

This best-loved Sea "Chantey" is based on the Minor Scale. Listen to my rendition on the recording, then give it a try. Playing a few easy Minor songs will help you learn the scale.

What	shall	we	do	with	a	drunk	en	sai	lor
6	6	6	6	6	6	6	4	5	6

What	shall	we	do	with	a	drunk	en	sai	lor
6	6	6	6	6	6	6	4	5	6

What	shall	we	do	with	a	drunk	en	sai	lor
6	6	6	6	6	6	6	7	7	8

Ear	ly	in	the	morn	ing	
7	6	6	5	4	4	

If you enjoyed this song, you can go to The Song Section, on page 86, and start playing any of the Minor Scale-based songs that you like.

Track 15: Dwahs and Wah-Wahs

Perhaps you noticed that my two versions of *Amazing Grace* at the beginning and the end of Track 13 were somewhat different. In the first (since I was not expecting you to play along, and wanted to show off a bit), I used *"hand wah wahs,"* two note chords instead of three note chords, and even single notes.

The Hand Wah Wah

Since the invention of the harmonica, players have used their hands to "shape" the sound. This involves closing the space in front of the harmonica to muffle or mute it, then opening that space for a brighter, louder, sound. The pictures will help you to understand the hand position, but only many years or even decades of practice will perfect this beautiful effect.

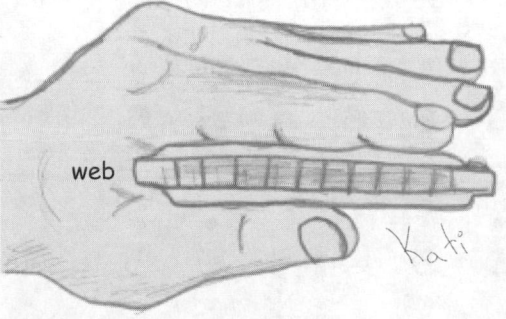

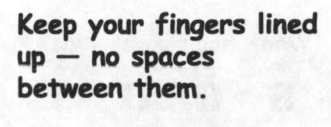

Keep your fingers lined up — no spaces between them.

web

The Left Handed Sandwich Grip

For the traditional wah-wah hand position, even left-handed players usually hold the harmonica in what I call the left handed sandwich hold.

Make sure that the harmonica is securely (but not painfully) pushed into the "web" of the left hand, between the thumb and forefinger. All of the fingers on top of the harp should be in a line and together — not fanned out or spread apart so that there are spaces between them.

The Right Position

The right hand is used to open and shut the air space in front of the harmonica. Most players get the best control by keeping the heels of the hands together, and the *ball* of the right thumb against the *side* of the left thumb. Try to get a good seal between the hands, but having a small open space between the hands on the side facing you is okay.

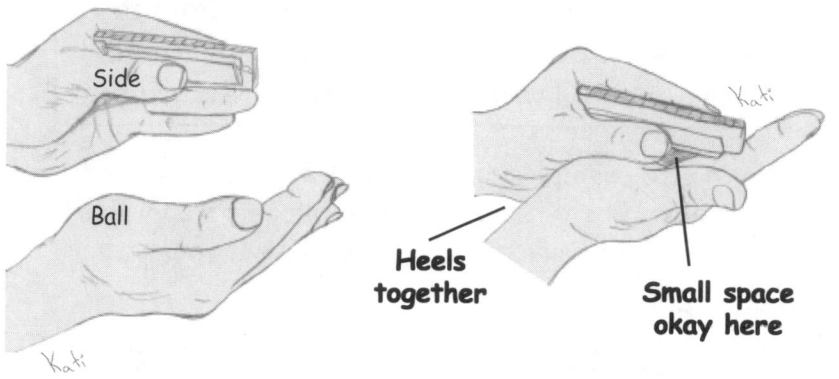

Unless you are very flexible, keep your elbows together — this will help you bend your right hand from the wrist when opening and closing that air space.

On the other hand (sorry), I've seen people with the oddest hand wah-wah positions get a great sound, so experiment until you find a hand position that suits you.

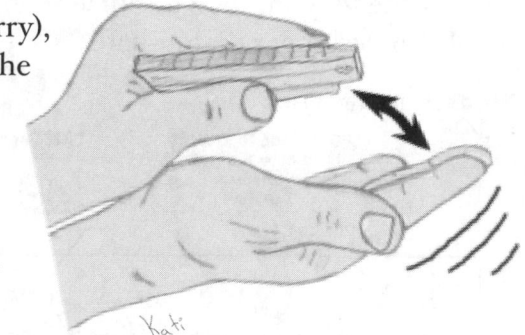

Hand Wah Speed

Hand "wahs" can be played as slowly as one wah (which is usually a closed position to open position) per beat. Or they can be played so fast that they merge into one fast, fluttering, motion (rather like the so-called Native American "war whoop," which was strictly, as I understand it, a Hollywood invention).

My Wah Demos

You can hear me, in the background, begin the song *Amazing Grace* by playing "A-maz-ing grace..." using chords with no wah-wah. Then I demonstrate some hand wah-wah technique on the single notes as I play "...how sweet the sound, to save a wretch, like me-ee-ee-ee."

> A line after the word "flutter" means hold the flutter until you reach the note under the end of the line. I'll write out slower ones as wahs.

I go on to give examples of slow hand wah-wahs on single notes 4 and 3. Then I do a more complicated wah wah riff. Try it yourself, but vary the timing to make it your own...

(Demonstrated
at :27)

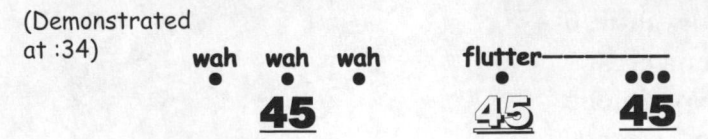

In my demonstration of the Chicago riff, I do three single wahs on the long in, then a "flutter" on the out and last in (which I hold longer than usual).

(Demonstrated
at :34)

> The key to a good hand wah-wah is to make sure than your hands block as much of the air as possible when in closed position, and block no air at all when open. Since everyone has different sized hands, everyone has a slightly different hand wah-wah position.

Wah-Wah Hints

Do at least some wah-wah practice in the bathroom, for three reasons. Firstly, the mirror will show you if your right hand is completely blocking the air, or if you are leaving "gaps." As I wrote and illustrated on page 49, a small space on the side *facing* you is okay.

But on the *back side?* Closed means closed — you don't want to see hands like these in the mirror! Get a good seal between those hands!

This is why we check our hand Wah-Wah in the mirror!

Secondly, the wah-wah sound projects outwards, away from you — it is more clearly heard by the listener than the player. Most bathrooms have lots of hard edges (like tile walls, and mirrors) that echo your wah-wah back to you. Stairwells and pedestrian tunnels are also good for wah-ing, and for playing in general — nice acoustics!

An Exercise That's All Wet

Lastly, here's a great hand wah-wah exercise. Put the fingers of your left hand over the fingers of your right hand, with the fingers at right angles to each other. Bring the heels of your hands together. This is the classic "use your hands to cup some water" position. It's also quite close to the ideal hand wah-wah position — if your hands will hold water, you've got a good seal between them. So cup a handful of water, and try to keep it from leaking out for as long as possible!

About Starting to Get Single Notes

If you haven't already experimented with getting the two hole chords described on page 34 in Track Ten, you'd probably better put in a few minutes on them right now. If you have, you're ready to start working on your single notes.

Actually, you may already have played a single note on the 1 hole, back in Track 11 on page 36. But the technique involved in getting any of the higher single notes is completely different.

To play a single note, you'll have to pucker your lips as though you were whistling, then push the harmonica slightly in between them.

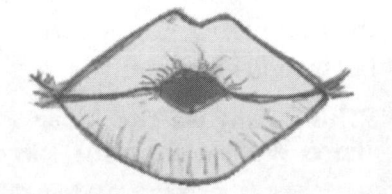

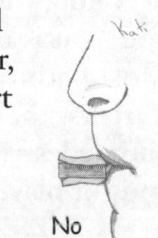

As always, the harmonica must be well under the upper lip and over the lower, or the flesh of your lips will block part of the hole, and give you a choked or muffled sound.

Yes   No

On the Tip of Your Tongue

During practice, use the tip of your tongue to locate the center of the hole that you're aiming at (of course, you can't do this while trying to play a song.)

> Don't worry if getting single notes is hard to do at first — it is — but there is nothing in this book that absolutely requires them. Just keep working on two hole chords (which will strengthen your pucker muscle, or *orbicularis oris*), and spend a few minutes a day trying to play using single notes.

The "Dwah" Effect

Say the word "dwah" (of course it's a word, at least for harp players). Now say it slowly, almost as a "doo-wah." Think about the motion of your tongue — it probably starts out touching the roof of your mouth just behind your front teeth, to prepare for the "duh" or d' sound of the dwah.

Air pressure builds up behind the tongue, and it tenses. Then, like a dam bursting, it drops down and back, to form the "doo" of the dwah, before returning to a normal, relaxed, position for the wah. Put the three parts together smoothly — "duh-oo-ah" — speed it up, and there's your dwah.

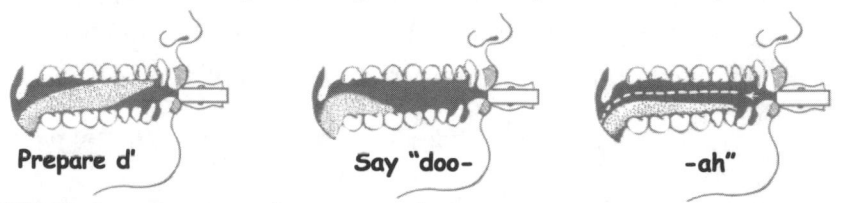

Prepare d'   Say "doo-   -ah"

While keeping your lips in single note or two note chord position (this is important, so don't let them open up on the "wah" of the dwah!), practice saying some dwahs. Now — and here's the tricky part — do it on the inhale!

Listen to my examples. Start empty. Keep your nose closed. Don't let your lips separate at all when you get to the "ah" part. Just make the exact same dwah tongue motion as you do on the out breath. Like everything else, it will feel strange at first but come with practice. Dwahs are most commonly used on the two hole chords 3 and 4, 4 and 5, and 5 and 6.

Dwah-ing the Boogie Woogie

Use a dwah on each in breath for more interesting Boogie Woogie riffs. Here's my first of two examples.

(Begins at 1:00)

dwah   dwah   dwah   dwah
 •   •   •   •   •   •   •   •   •
45   4̲5̲   **34**   4̲5̲   **45**   4̲5̲   **34**

And here's my second Boogie Woogie example.

(Begins at 1:05)

The Dwah-da and the Dirty Dogs

Dwahs also add some bite to your Dirty Dog riffs, as in my examples. When doing a series of dwahs in swing beat, I often alternate each dwah with a da — it helps to swing the beat, since the da is faster to say than the dwah (and in a swing the first part of the beat lasts longer than the second, as you no doubt recall). So in these examples (or any Dirty Dog riffs that you want to use dwahs on), I am articulating (whispering):

•   •   •   •

dwah   da   dwah   da   dwah   **(silent beat)**

dirr	d'	dirr	d'	dog	(Demonstrated on
dwah	da	dwah	da	dwah	Track 15 at 1:10)
•		•		•	
45	**45**	**45**	**45**	**45**	**(silent beat)**

dirr	d'	dirr	d'	dog	
dwah	da	dwah	da	dwah	
•		•		•	•
45	**45**	**56**	**56**	**67**	

Add a dwah to the last in note (before the three beat silence) of a Chicago Breathing Pattern — it sounds great! And you'll use some dwahs in the rock and roll "bridge" on the next track.

I'm sorry to keep "harping" on the subject.
But I cannot emphasize enough that this
method relies heavily on listening and doing.
So if you tend to be primarily a reader, please
remember to use the CD, as well...

Track 16: Some Easy Hard Rock

By the time you finish this track, you'll be able to play a
Twelve Bar rock and roll solo similar to the one in my intro,
including a rock and roll "bridge."

The Rock and Roll Bridge

A "bridge" is a piece of music that comes in between two
pieces of music that are similar to each other. It's often the
most dramatic (and loudest) part of a music verse. In this
case, we'll use a bridge to connect two of my favorite rock
and roll Breathing Patterns. I'll write this eight beat, two bar
bridge down with dwahs, but you can vary it by using one wah
per beat, or a flutter wah — or all of the above!

(Begins at :045)   **Try dwahs and flutters at the same time!**

dwah   dwah   dwah   dwah
  •   •   •   •   •   • • •
45   45   45   45   45   (3 silent beats)

Dave's Favorite Rock Breathing Pattern

Memorize this two bar breathing pattern, starting with
practice in the middle of the harmonica. Use some dahs on
the in breaths, to make them nice and clear. But emphasize
the out breaths — make them crisp and forceful — to give
this Breathing Pattern a real rock and roll feel, since rock and
roll usually emphasizes the second and fourth beat of every bar.
Try it first on a two (or three) hole chord in the middle.

Don't forget the two beats of silence at the end of the pattern!

  •   •   •   •   •   •   • •
in in out   in in out   in in out in

(1:30)
  •   •   •   •   •   •   • •
45 45   45   45 45   45   45 45   45 45

Five Rock Riff Demos   (All five demonstrated 2:00 - 2:40)

Once you own this Breathing Pattern, apply it in a variety of places, along with my verbal instructions. In my examples I'll start you on the 1, 2, and 3 hole chord — keep it wide and open to avoid the choked sound.

123 **123** 1̲2̲3̲ **123** **123** 1̲2̲3̲ **123123** 1̲2̲3̲ **123** ˙ ˙

Then you'll start moving it around. I'll mostly notate these as two note chords, but use three if you need to, and don't worry about the exact notes, except when you end on the 1 in. Watch those silent beats!

Low to High Rock Riff

23 **23** 3̲4̲ **34** **34** 5̲6̲ **567** **567** 6̲7̲8̲ **910** ˙ ˙

High to Way Low Rock Riff (a cool ending for a verse)

910 **910** 8̲9̲ **45** **45** 4̲5̲ **23** **23** 2̲3̲ **1** ˙ ˙

Jump Outs to the Middle Rock Riff (in slide down to the last low in)

23 **23** 4̲5̲ **23** **23** 4̲5̲ **23** **23** 4̲5̲ **12** ˙ ˙

34 Dwah Rock Riff

dwah dwah   dwah dwah   dwah dwah   dwah   ˙ ˙
34 **34** 4̲5̲ **34** **34** 4̲5̲ **34** **34** 4̲5̲ **34**

Don't Get Discouraged — This Took Me Four Years!

Now apply this pattern *anywhere* you like, shaking and sliding, wahing and dwahing. Make it crisp, and don't forget the silences! Don't get discouraged if some of these seem hard — as I said, I was playing for four years before I could do this well (and how long have you been playing so far?).

Twelve Bar Rock & Roll Solos: A Recipe for Success

Our Rock Breathing Pattern and the Bridge are both two bars long. So we can easily improvise a Twelve Bar rock solo by combining six of them. This is the order to do it in:

Four Rock Breathing Patterns

One Rock Bridge

One Last Rock Breathing Pattern (often high to very low)

You can use any notes or special effects that you like on the Rock Breathing Patterns, and this *"recipe"* for a Twelve Bar rock solo will always work!

The First Demo Rock Verse   (Begins at 3:20)

The first of my two examples is very simple, although it sounds great. You can see how both of these verses fit the Twelve Bar rock solo recipe.

123 123 123 123 123 123 123123 123 123 ••

123 123 123 123 123 123 123123 123 123 ••

45 45 45 45 45 45 45 45 45 45 ••

123 123 123 123 123 123 123123 123 123 ••

Get empty for the Bridge!

Flutter
• • • •   •   •   •   •
45   45

123 123 123 123 123 123 123123 123 123 ••

As I've mentioned before — the notation for the following rock solo, as well as the one on the previous page, *looks* complicated. Playing the actual solos while listening to my verbal instruction is far easier, since they're both based on simple Breathing Patterns...

The Second Demo Rock Verse   (Begins at 3:50)

23 23 45 23 23 45 23 23 45 23

23 23 45 23 23 45 23 23 45 23

dwah dwah   dwah dwah   dwah dwah   dwah
45   45   45   34   34   45   45   45   45   34

23 23 45 45 45 56 56 56 56 45

                 dwah dwah dwah dwah
Get empty for
the Bridge!   45   45   45   45   45

89 89 56 45 45 45 23 23 23 1

That's rockin'! And now might be a good time to visit Playalong Track 23 — The Classic Rock Playalong — and make up some solos of your own.

Track 17: The Rhymin' Blues

In my humble opinion, the master skill — the most important ability that a human being can attain — is the ability to control one's own mind and emotions. As I discuss in the recording, the *"Dozens,"* or Rhyming Blues, is a prime example of this. To me the very genesis of the blues was an attempt to achieve mental mastery by turning angst into art — transforming the pain of slavery and second-class citizenship into some of the most creative forms of music that the world has ever known.

A Hundred Years of the Rhymin' Blues Riff

This riff and its variations has inspired hundreds of artists, from Muddy Waters in the '40s to Janis Joplin in the 60's to J. Geils in the 70's to rapper Nas' new hit "Bridgin' the Gap" in 2005. Practice the Breathing Pattern on the middle holes first. Make sure you don't play during the silent beats — they're reserved for your lyrics! Start after the count of three:

(1:40)

in   **out**   **in**   **in**   (two silent beats)

456   **456**   **456**   **456**   (two silent beats)

Simplified Timing (with three times as many beats)

Timing seems difficult? Play it with a tripled beat as in the lines *below.* Once you can, keep playing, but look up at the lines *above,* and tap your foot four times instead of twelve.

(Larger dots show the "real" beat, but tap once for all twelve dots.)

in   **out**   **in**   **in**   (seven silent beats)

456   **456**   **456**   **456**   (seven silent beats)

If you continue to have any problems with the timing of this riff, listen — lots — to my recorded examples.

The Low Down Rhymin' Blues Riff

If you've worked at getting good tone from your low end notes, try it down there — nice and low and mellow.

(2:25)

123   **123**   **123**   **123** (two silent beats)

Or with simplified timing:

123   **123**   **123**   **123** (seven silent beats)

The Real Rhymin' Blues Riff

After you've mastered the Rhymin' Blues Riff on the middle and low holes, try taking it where it belongs, with a dwah aimed at the 3, or the 3 and 4 holes.

(3:25)

123   **345**   dwah **34**   **123** (two silent beats)

Or with simplified timing:

123   **345**   dwah **34**   **123** (seven silent beats)

You might even want to try it with single notes:

2   **4**   dwah **3**   **2** (two silent beats)

Finish it Off with a...Shake!

I like to end this type of song with a shake on the 4 and 5 in.

Fancier Variations of the Rhymin' Blues Riff

There are many. For example, an extra 4 in or 345 in can be added, for a slightly different Rhymin' Riff (the first one I demonstrate when discussing the variations) similar to that used in my *Bad Olympics* intro and the song *Bad to the Bone,* by George Thorogood (and lately a rap favorite).

(4:00)

123 345 345 34 123   (two silent beats)

Or, with simplified timing, single notes, and my intro lyrics:

2 4 4 3 2 You're the bad- dest of bad

Ready-Made Blues/Rap Style Songs

You can flatter your friends or dis your enemies, entertain your co-workers, and leave the world's greatest answering machine messages — just by inserting a name into these ready-made rhymin' Blues. To keep the beat right, you may need to "adjust" the number of syllables in the name, so a David might become a Dave, and a Jennifer might need to be a Jen.

You can use the simplest middle hole two beat version, or the fanciest. I'll write the 2 in-4 out-4 in- 3 in-2 in riff in the parentheses, but you can put whichever riff you like into the two beats of riff that alternate with the lyrics. Just remember, when singing, that the syllable under the dot gets emphasized, the other syllables fall in between the beats.

On the next page you'll find a slight variation on the song I use during the intro to this track. You can use it yourself as a "fill-in-the-blanks" song that can be either a roast or a toast, depending on how the listener interprets the word "bad." Listen to my Rhymin' Blues on the recording for help with the timing, then play and sing one for a pal who needs a lift!

Not a singer? Play this riff for someone who is — they'll love it!

The Bad Olympics: A Fill-in-the-Blanks Rhymin' Blues

(2 4 4 3 2)   *(Dave's)*   the   bad-   dest   of   bad

(2 4 4 3 2)   You   just   lis-   ten   to   me

(2 4 4 3 2)   'cause *(his/her)*   mid-   dle   name

(2 4 4 3 2)   Is   spell'd   B-   A-   D

(2 4 4 3 2)   Be-   cause   *(s)he's*   so   Ba- ad

(2 4 4 3 2)   If   the   truth   must   be   told

(2 4 4 3 2)   At   the   Baaad   O-   lym-   pics

(2 4 4 3 2)   *(S)he'd*   go home   with the go-old   **(45)** _{wwwww}

A Love or Friendship Rhymin' Blues (not on recording)

(2 4 3 2)   You   know   when   I'm   feel-   in'

(2 4 3 2)   So   down   —   an' far a-way

(2 4 3 2)   The   thought   of   *(Kate's)* face
                                                  (your friend ship)

(2 4 3 2)   Blows   my   Blues   far   a- way   **(45)** _{wwwww}

To create a song of your own, think of two rhyming words and the idea that connects them. Then create a four line "poem," in which lines two and four rhyme. Throw your riff in before each line, end with a 45 shake, and you've got it!

Track 18: More Folk Songs, and Playing By Ear

The key (if you'll pardon the pun) to playing by ear is to know the Major Scale — backwards and forwards, up and down — until you can play it in your sleep! So you'll begin this track by learning to play the full Major Scale, with the two notes that we've left out so far.

The Full Major Scale

Here it is. The shift in Breathing Pattern from out-in on holes 4, 5, and 6 to in-out on 7 will fool you, at first. Play it both from low to high, and high to low. I'll write this out in single notes, but just aim and play chords if you can't go single!

4	**4**	5	**5**	6	**6**	7	7	
C	D	E	F	G	A	B	C	(1:00)
do	re	mi	fa	so	la	ti	do	

I've also included the letter names of these notes (as played on our key of C harmonicas, as well as the "solfege" (do-re-mi) names. Since this Major Scale starts on a "C" note, it's called a *"C Major Scale,"* or a *"Major Scale in the key of C."* If you're interested in why music works as it does, read about my book *Music Theory Made Easy* in the "Where to Go from Here" section.

The Case of the Missing Notes

In order to make all the harmonica's notes, well, harmonious — two notes of the Major Scale were omitted from the low end, and one from the high end. (Want all the details? You'll find them in my *Music Theory Made Easy for Harmonica*). On the next page is a diagram that shows this. Notice that there is no F or A note in the low end, and no B in the high end.

The ABC's of the Harmonica

Hole #:	1	2	3	4	5	6	7	8	9	10
Out notes:	C	E	G	C	E	G	C	E	G	C
In notes:	D	G	B	D	F	A	B	D	F	A

We've already learned to compensate for this. When playing *Amazing Grace,* it would be nice *not* to have to make those 4 in to 6 in jumps. But try playing it using the low end:

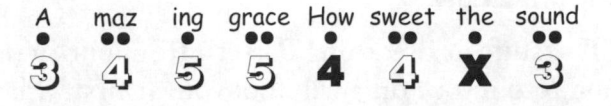

A	maz	ing	grace	How	sweet	the	sound
3	4	5	5	4	4	X	3

Unless you can "bend" notes, an advanced technique used mostly by Blues players, it can't be done. The note for "the" — an "A" note — is not there for you in the low end, although it's perfectly accessible up at 6 in. Pretty much anytime you see a song of mine with a 4 in to 6 in jump — like *Amazing Grace, Danny Boy, Red River Valley,* or many others — the jump is there to avoid a missing note in the low end.

The Jumping Major Scale

Some songs need to start on the note 4 out and head down, Practicing this scale will eliminate the "Where the heck is that note?" problem that plagues most beginning harmonica players — and discourages many from continuing. Play it with chords or single notes — it'll work fine either way.

(1:55)

4	3	6	6	5	5	4	4
C	B	A	G	F	E	D	C

Following are two great songs that will hone your real life Major Scale skills!

Oh When the Saints   (At Very Beginning of this track)

In the intro to this track, I threw a few extra flourishes (like the ending, in parentheses) into this great Dixieland tune, mostly during the long notes and silences at the end of lines. It can be played slow or fast. In fact, in New Orleans it's often used at funerals, played slowly on the way to the cemetery to mourn the deceased, and fast on the way back, to celebrate his or her life!

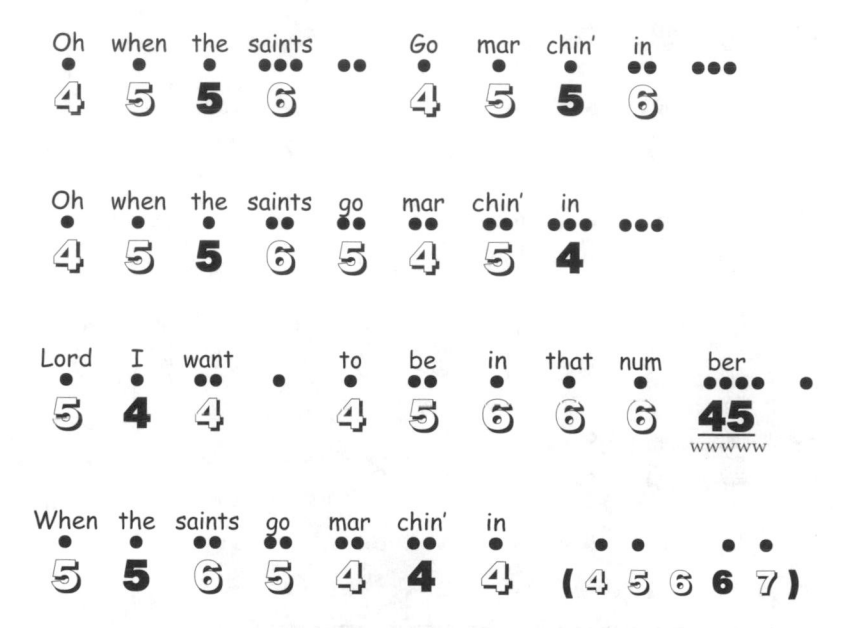

If the ending (in parens) seems a bit much, just hold the last 4 out note for five beats, fading it towards the end...

Beethoven's Ninth, The Ode to Joy

Much classical music is based on the Major Scale, although the Minor Scale is also used. In fact, lots of classical music is actually based on earlier folk tunes, so the line between folk and classical music is blurred, as is the line between Blues and rock. You can hear the first part of the Fourth Movement of *Beethoven's Ninth Symphony* — also known as the hymn *Joyful Joyful We Adore You* and the *Ode to Joy* — at the end of this track.

The Fourth Movement of the Ninth Symphony

(First two lines only at 2:15)

Now go to The Song Section, and play!

Figuring Out Songs "by Ear"

On the next page are the first lines of a few songs based on the Major Scale. Choose one and and look at the first note only. Play the Major Scale a few times, then see if you can figure out the rest of the notes of the song, one at a time.

Just ask yourself: "Should the next note sound higher, lower, or the same?" Then try it — if that note doesn't work — try a different one! You may find it useful to write each note down (like 4 out-3 in etc.) as you locate them by trial and error.

As many songs have repeated sections, it goes faster than you'd expect! And if you absolutely can't find a note that seems like it should be lower than 4 out, it is most probably a missing note, so try jumping up to the 6 in, or less likely, the 5 in.

If this seems hard at first, play the entire first line of the song, then try to figure out the rest of the song.

I come on	theSloop John B.	My gran fa ther an me
3 5 5	5 5 5 5	3 5 5 5 5 5

Frer e Jac que	Frer e Jac que	Dor mezvous?	Dor mezvous
4 4 5 4	4 4 5 4	5 5 6	5 5 6

Fran kie and John nie were lo vers	Lor dy but howthey did love
4 5 6 6 6 5 4 4	4 5 6 6 6 5 4

Jin gle bells	jin gle bells	jin gle all the way	oh whatfun
5 5 5	5 5 5	5 6 4 4 5	5 5 5

Mi chaelrow the boat a shore	Hal le liu yah	Mich ael row the
4 5 6 5 6 6 6	5 6 6 6	5 6 6 5

No Notes to Start With...

If you don't even know the first note, but suspect that the song is based on the Major Scale, try this: play (yes, again) the Major Scale a few times. Then think about the song.

If the song starts *high* and works its way down *lower* in the first few notes, try using 6 out as the first note, then use the "By Ear" strategy I just described. Can't seem to find the next note? Try starting on 7 out. If the song starts *low* and works its way *up*, try 4 out as a first note. If that doesn't work, try 3 out, then 5 out. As a last resort, try 3 in or 2 in...

Track 19: Putting it All Together

There's not really too much to say about this track, except: *Congratulations!* If you've made it this far, you can play more than I could after years of teaching myself. Luckily, I'm a better harp teacher now! Where was I, back when I needed me?

A Playalong Hint

Spend lots of time with the Playalong Tracks. Use the Breathing Patterns that you know before learning the new ones in Track 20. Play what you play with zest and feeling, even if you can't play much.

Ideas for Other Breathing Pattern Combinations

Put the Breathing Patterns together in different ways — either with or without the playalong music. Maybe a Boogie Woogie Breathing Pattern plus eight beats of Train Wheel would sound cool. And could a bar of in Dirty Dogs then a bar of out Dirty Dogs replace the Rock Bridge in a rock solo?

Try anything — be creative in putting together what you know! Combine a Boogie Woogie with a Rock Bridge. Or try fitting three quarters of a bar of the new Dirty Dogs from Track 20 (lose the last silent beat) into the the three beats of silence at the end of a Rock Bridge (below) or a Chicago Riff (not shown):

● ● ● ●　　● 　　●　　●　　●

innnn　out　　**in**　out　**in**　out　**in**　　(Not demonstrated, see Track 20 for new Dirty Dog riff)

Forget and Forgive, Once in a While

Once in a while, forget everything you know and just blow! Promise yourself, in advance, that you're going to make mistakes and just keep going. If you do this with the Playalong Tracks, keep just one thing in mind — when in doubt, inhale. Inhaling anywhere will always fit in when playing Blues or rock, if you put feeling and rhythm into it!

Track 20: A Few More BP's

If you feel comfortable using the breathing patterns that you already know, you're ready to vary them, and learn new ones!

Seven Boogie Woogie Breathing Pattern Variations

Simply by changing the timing of our standard Boogie Woogie Breathing Pattern — lengthening some breaths, and shortening others — we create more interesting variations.

Here are a few favorites. A new timing notation (half a beat, then a beat and a half) indicates a short breath followed by a long one. Listen to my seven examples on the recording, to get the feel of these. Most end with one beat of in breath, followed by a silent beat. Please create variations of your own, and play them using slides, shakes, dwahs, or hand wah wahs on any holes you like!

$\frac{1}{2}$ $1\frac{1}{2}$

(:02)
#1) **in** **out** **in** **out** **in** **out** **in**

(:07)
#2) **in** **out** **in** **out** **in** **out** **in**

(:11)
#3) **in** **out** **in** **out** **in** **out** **in**

(:15 & :19)
#4 & 5) **in** **out** **in** **out** **in** **out** **in**

(:23)
#6) **in** **out** **in** **out** **in** **out** **in**

(:28)
#7) **in** **out** **in** **out** **in** **out** **in**

> You can improvise on the timing of the breathing patterns themselves — Try it!

Dirty Dirty Dog In & Out Variations

Now we come to the "real" use of the Dirty Dog rhythm.
Instead of using all inhales or all exhales, you'll use the basic
rhythm as an in and out swinging Breathing Pattern.
Naturally, you can move it around and add effects like shakes,
slides, wahs and dwahs, as in my examples on the CD. You'll
usually do two of these one bar riffs in a row.

(At :38 of
Track 20)

dirrr	d'	dirrr	d'	dog	
•		•		•	•
in	out	**in**	out	**in**	(silent)

The Chicago Dog

Take the first two beats of the previous Breathing Pattern,
and substitute them for the first two beats of the Chicago
Breathing Pattern. Don't forget the three silent beats!

•		•		•		•	• • •
in	out	**in**	out	**in**	out	**in**	

(At :55 of
Track 20)

Another Great 16 Beat Breathing Pattern

Take two new one bar Dirty Dog Patterns, and add one of the
Chicago Dog Patterns — you'll produce a four bar Breathing
Pattern that can be used to create fine riffs without limit. Try
this example, from the beginning of Verse Two of Track 22:

•	•	•	•
34 45	**45** 56	**56**	

(Hear this at :38
of Track 22)

•	•	•	•
slide up 56	**45** 45	**34**	

dwah

•	•	•	•	•	• • •
34 45	**45** 56	**56** 56	**45**		

wwwwwwwwwwwwwwwwwwwwwwwwwwwwww **slidedown**

Make up lots of your own, with slides, shakes, wahs, dwahs —
whatever you can think of (or do without thinking).

Heavy Rock Boogie Riff

If you liked the Rock Boogie in Track 10 and Playalong Track 24, you can learn to play a version of it on the harmonica. I'll demonstrate three versions here, and at the beginning of Playalong Track 24. The first is easy, the second and third get harder — keep a steady and swingin' beat and play 'em over and over, either by yourself or along with Track 24, as I do.

(At 1:40 of Track 20 and beginning of Track 24)

dah dah dwah
2 2 3 4

The third line can be played in two ways.

As written in **black**, it's a two bar riff with three silent beats.

dah da d' dwah
2 2 2 **3** 4

Or you can use this 2 in after the in slide as the first note of a new bar of **2 2** 2 **3** 4 **in slide** (Add the grey notes)

dah da d' dwah
2 2 2 **3** 4 **in slide** **2** (**2** 2 **3** 4 **in slide**)

A Good C & W Breathing Pattern

If you like C & W music try playing this simple four bar breathing pattern along with Country Playalong Track 25.

It's got one tricky timing part: a short breath (half beat) followed by a longer breath (whole beat) then another half beat.

Listen to it at 1:50 on this Track, and use it to play along with Track 25, too. You might want to check out *C & W Harmonica Made Easy,* if you're serious about this kind of music!

half whole half
in in out in **in in out in**

in in out in out in

Track 21: R & B Stress Buster

Focusing your complete attention onto your breathing will reduce stress, as discussed on the CD in this track. Just play this basic R & B Riff, getting *totally empty* by the end of each out breath, and *totally filled up* by the end of each in breath.

$$\overset{\bullet\bullet}{\underline{\mathbf{123}}} \quad \overset{\bullet\bullet}{\underline{\mathbf{456}}} \quad \overset{\bullet\bullet}{\underline{\mathbf{456}}} \quad \overset{\bullet\bullet}{\underline{\mathbf{456}}}$$

If you're in a slightly more active mood, you can play Chicago and Boogie Woogie breathing patterns — slowly and mindfully — along with this R & B background. But whatever you play, make sure that you keep your attention focused tightly on your breathing, because that's what relaxes you.

> Track 21 will relax and focus you. Tracks 22 - 25 will provide you with a more active mental workout that will focus your attention, hyper-oxygenate your brain, and be lots of fun!

Track 22: Guitar Blues Playalong

A single blues guitar player makes a great accompaniment for a harp player! My first harp verse of Track 22 demonstrates the use of the Boogie Woogie "Variations" from Track 20.

My second verse demonstrates the new Dirty Dog patterns from Track 20.

My third and fourth verses demonstrate "**Blues Scale**" use. The Blues Scale (see page 83) — like the Major Scale and Minor Scale — is a "musical alphabet," in this case, for Blues Music.

Verse three (written out for you on page 85) is based on the Simplified Blues Scale, and will be challenging but playable. Verse four is based on the "Real" Blues Scale. It's too hard for you to play now, but it'll show you where you want to go!

Track 23: Classic Rock Playalong

The band gets down here, expecially the drummer! Use the Rock Solo Recipe from page 58 to create your own verses, or use any of the Breathing Patterns you know to play riffs that will work with this rockin' background music.

Verse Two demonstrates the Rock Breathing Pattern from Track 16, and Verse Three adds some "bending." If this style appeals to you, check out *"Instant Blues Harmonica"* — it features more info on improvising strategy using this type of riff.

Track 24: Blues Rock Boogie

You're welcome to join me at the beginning of this track in playing the three different Rock Boogie Riffs from page 74. Or you can use any of the Breathing Patterns to play along, as I also do. Need more inspiration? The ends of both Tracks 10 and 11 (pages 34 and 37) will help.

Track 25: C & W Playalong

Use the C & W breathing pattern from page 71 along with this playalong track. When you can get single notes, you can try the "Country Improv Scale" below (play it up and down), or check out my *C & W Harmonica Made Easy* (page 93).

1 2 2 3 4 5 6

> Most of the Breathing Patterns you've learned can be used with most of these tracks. Review Track 19 for some playalong hints, and remember to use your stereo control to lose my demonstration solos, if you like. Turn the lights low, the volume of your CD high, and Enjoy!

The Song Section

Here are some great songs to play, based on the **Major** Scale. If you've already listened to and read Track 13, you should be able to play all of these songs (although checking out Track 18 wouldn't hurt). Don't worry about getting single notes — just aim your lips at the right hole and keep track of your ins and outs. Start with the ones that "you can hear in your head" — the better you know a song, the easier it will be to play it on your harmonica. Use shakes and wahs and dwahs, as you like.

Red River Valley (Notice the jump to avoid a low missing note)

On Top of Old Smoky

(Please read about using the "big and little dots" at the top of page 80)

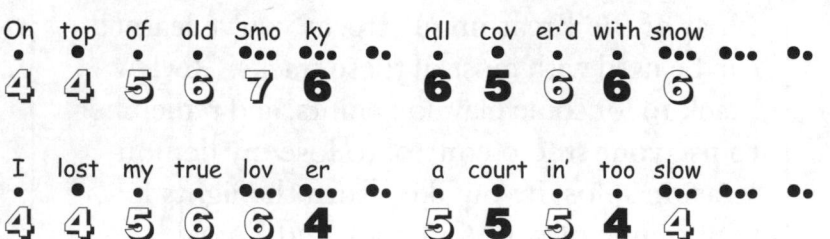

Oh Shenandoah

Oh	Shen	an	doah	I	long	to	see	you
•	•		••		•			••
3	4	4	4	4	5	5	6	6

Far	a	way	you	lone	some	ri	ver
•		•••		•			••
7	7	6	6	6	6	5	6

Oh	Shen	an	doah	I	want	to	see	you
•	•		••		•		•	••
6	6	6	6	5	6	5	4	4

A	way	•	I'm	gone	a	way	•
•	••					••	
3	4		4	5	6	6	

'cross	the	wide	Mis	sour	ri	•
•		••			••	
4	4	5	4	4	4	

> **Just remember:**
> **Breathe OUT on**
> **Outlined numbers!**

Morning Has Broken

(Again: Please see page 80 to learn about "triple time" dots)

Morn	ing	has	bro	ken	like	the	first	mor	or	ning	•
•	•	•	•••	•••	•	•	•	•••	•••	••	
4	5	6	7	8	7	6	6	6	7	6	

Black	bird	is	sing	ing		like	the	first	bird		
•	•	•	•••	•••	•••	•	•	•	•••	•••	•••
4	4	5	6	6		6	5	4	4	7	7

Praise	for	his	sing	ing		Praise	for	the	mor	ning	
•	•	•	•••	•••	•••	•	•	•	•••	•••	•••
6	5	6	7	6		6	5	4	4	4	

Praise	for	them	spring	ing		fresh	from	the	word		
•	•	•	•••	•••	•••	•	••	•	•••	•••	•••
5	4	5	6	6		4	5	4	4		

Blow the Man Down

Now all you young sai lors that fol low the sea
5 6 6 6 5 4 5 6 6 6 5

With a Yo! Ho! Blow the man down!
4 5 6 6 5 5 5 4

Now please pay at ten tion and lis ten to me
3 4 5 4 3 2 3 4 5 4 3

And give me a chance to blow the man down!
4 6 6 6 6 5 5 4 5 4

Home on the Range (Jumps around a lot to avoid missing notes)

Oh give me a home where the buf- fa- lo roam
7 6 7 8 8 7 7 6 5 5 5

Where the deer and the an- te- lope play
5 5 6 4 4 4 3 4 4

And sel- dom is heard a dis- cour- a- ging word
3 3 4 4 5 7 7 6 5 5 5

and the skies are not cloud- y all day
5 5 5 4 4 3 4 4 4

Home Home on the Range Where the deer...
6 5 5 4 5 3 3 4

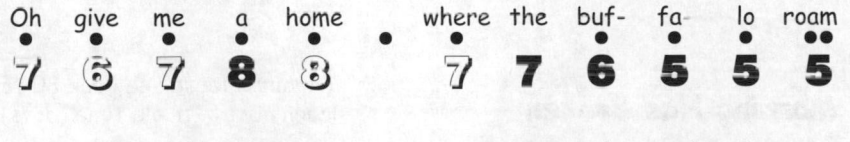
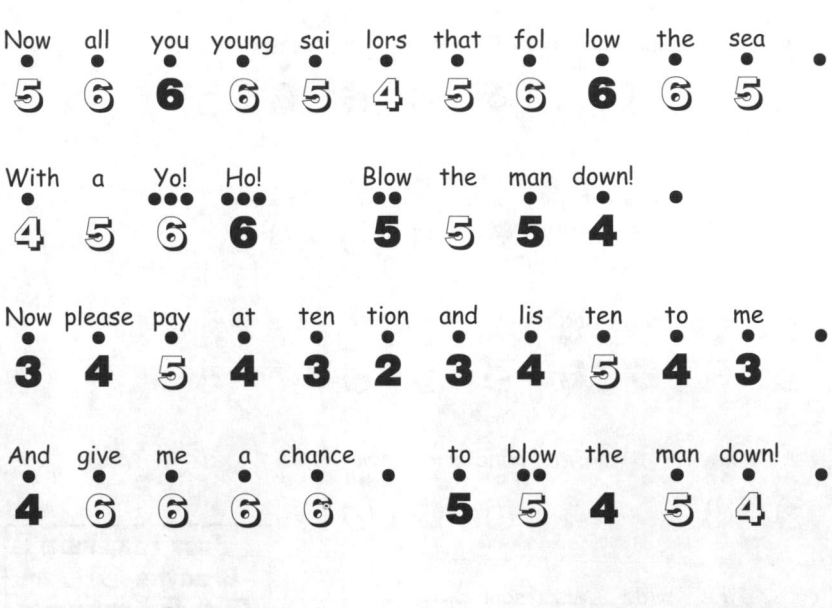

Go to 4th note of line 2 and play to end of line 4

Brahms Lullaby

5 5 6 5 5 6 5 6 7 7 6 6 6

4 5 5 4 4 5 5 4 5 7 6 6 7 7

4 4 7 6 5 6 5 4 5 6 6 5 6

4 4 7 6 5 6 5 4 5 5 4 4

He's Got The Whole World In His Hands

He's got the whole world in his hands
6 6 5 6 4 6 6 6

He's got the whole world in his hands
5 5 5 5 4 5 6 5

He's got the whole world in his hands
6 6 5 6 4 6 6 6

He's got the whole world in his hands
6 6 6 6 5 5 4 4

Notice the "one half then one and a half" beat timing in this lovely Spiritual song.

$\frac{1}{2}$ $1\frac{1}{2}$

A Good Morning to You

(Originally written in the 1800's, this melody was later used for "the birthday song.")

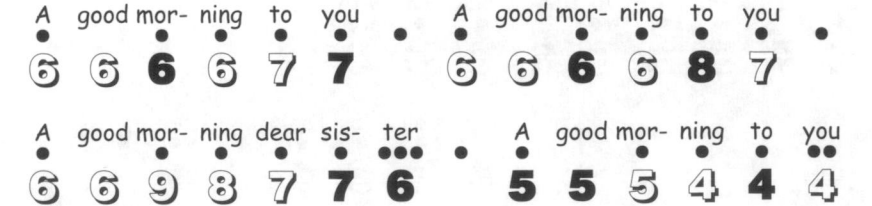

A good mor- ning to you   A good mor- ning to you
6 6 6 6 7 7   6 6 6 6 8 7

A good mor- ning dear sis- ter   A good mor- ning to you
6 6 9 8 7 7 6   5 5 5 4 4 4

Oh Danny Boy

Oh Dan ny boy . the Ker ry pipes are ca all ing .
3 4 4 5 4 5 6 6 5 4 4 6

from glen to glen and down the moun tain side
3 4 4 5 6 6 5 4 5 4

The sum mer's gone and all the flow'rs are dy yy ing .
3 4 4 5 4 5 6 6 5 4 4 6

'Tis you 'tis you must go 'tis I 'tis I must bide
3 4 4 5 6 6 5 4 4 6 7 7

But come ye back when sum mers in the mea ea ea dow .
6 6 7 7 7 7 6 6 6 6 5 4 4

Or when the val leys hush'd and white wi' snow .
6 6 7 7 7 7 6 6 5 4

'Tis I'll be there in sun light or in sha a a dow
6 6 6 8 8 8 7 6 7 6 5 4 4

Oh Dan ny boy oh Dan ny boy I love you so
3 4 4 5 6 6 5 4 4 6 7 7

Oh Susannah

(These songs may look scary, but they're easy
because you've heard them so many times!)

Oh I went to Al a ba ma with
4 4 5 6 6 6 6 5 4

my ban jo on my knee .
4 5 5 4 4 4

An I'm bound for Lou si an a now
4 4 5 6 6 6 6 5 4

my true love for to see
4 5 5 4 4 4

Oh Su san nah now don't you cry for me
5 5 6 6 6 6 6 5 4 4

Cuz I'm bound for Lou si an a now my true love for to see
4 4 5 6 6 6 5 4 4 5 5 4 4 4

Goodbye Old Paint

I'm rid ing Old Paint   I'm lead ing Old Dan
3 4 4 4 3   3 4 4 4 3

I'm off to Chey en ne to do the hoo li han
3 4 4 4 4 4 4 5 4 5 4 4

My foot's in the stir rup my po o ny won't stand
4 4 4 4 4 4 4 5 4 5 4 4

Good bye Old Pai nt I'm leav ing Chey enne
3 3 3 3 4 3 4 4 4 4

Good bye Old Pai nt I'm leav ing Chey enne
4 3 3 3 4 3 4 4 4 4

Notice the one half to one and a half beat timing in the last two lines of *Old Paint*.

$\frac{1}{2}$ $1\frac{1}{2}$

A Bluegrass Classic: Gary Owen (With "Big & Small Dots")

While learning this bluegrass classic, you can tap your foot once for *every* dot, large or small. But it will sound better if you tap only on the larger dots, for "triplet" timing (three notes per beat). You'll play Part One, then Part Two, then Part One again (with a different last note, as explained below).

Part One

7 7 6 6 5 5 4 4 5 4 5 5

7 7 6 6 5 5 4 4 4 3 4 4

7 7 6 6 5 5 4 4 5 4 5 5

6 6 6 7 7 6 5 4 (4)

The first time you play Part One, use this silent beat *instead* of the gray 4 out note in parentheses.

Part Two

5 5 6 5 6 5 6 5 6

7 7 6 5 6 5 6 5 6

7 7 8 8 8 7 7 6 6

6 6 6 7 7 6 5 4   (Go to beginning of Part One)

After playing Part Two, repeat Part One. This time, play the gray 4 out in parentheses, *instead* of playing the silent beat as you did the first time.

More Bluegrass: The Arkansaw Traveler

As a bluegrass tune, this is meant to be played fast! After you learn to play it while tapping your foot for each dot, big or small, try it using just the big dots (four notes per beat).

Far and far a way out in Ar kan saw
7 8 **8** 7 **6** **6** **6** 6 6 7

therelived a squat ter with a stub born jaw
7 **8** **8** 8 8 **8** 8 **8** 7 **6**

His nose was ru by red and his whis kers gray
6 7 8 **8** 7 **6** **6** **6** 6 6 7 .

He could sit and fid dle all the night and all the day
7 **7** 7 6 **6** 7 6 **5** 5 4 **4** 3 4 .

Came a trav ler down the road and ask'd if he couldfind a bed
6 **5** 5 6 **5** 5 **4** 5 **5** 4 4 5 **4** **3** **2**

"Yes, try the road" the kind ly squat ter said
4 4 4 **4** **4** 5 **4** 4 5 **4**

"Couldyou say how far the townmight be I'd
5 **5** 6 5 5 6 **5** 5 **4** 5

like to know 'fore I be gin"
5 **4** 4 5 **4** **3** **2**

"Quite a lit tle ways I rec kon tho I've nev er been"
7 **7** 7 6 **6** 7 6 **5** 5 4 **4** 3 4 .

The Star Spangled Banner

This song uses "partial bends." Bends (little "b" symbols) are like "dwahing" (page 53) on the 2 in note. As you know, the 2 in can give you a "choked" sound (page 39). Here, you *want* to get that choked, or "bent" sound! If bending notes, a great Blues technique, interests you, see my book on the subject (page 94).

O-	oh	say	can	you	see	by	the	dawn's	ear-	ly	light
3	2	1	2	3	4	5	4	4	2	2b	3

What	so	proud-	ly	we	hail'd	at	the	twi-light's	last	gleam-	ing
3	3	5	4	4	3	6	7	7	7	6	5	4

Whose	broad	stripes	and	bright	stars,	thro	the	per	i	lous	fight
3	2	1	2	3	4	5	4	4	2	2b	3

O'er	the	ram-	parts	we	watch'd	were	so	gal-	lant-	ly	stream-	ing
6	6	8	8	7	7	6	7	7	7	6	5	4

And	the	rock-	ets	red	glare	The	bombs	burst-	ing	in	air
5	5	5	5	6	6	5	5	4	5	5	5

Gave	proof	thru	the	night	that	our	flag	was	still	there
5	5	4	4	7	6	7	4	2	2b	3

O	say	does	tha-	at	Star	Span-	gled
6	7	7	7	7	6	6	6

Ba-	a-	ne-	er	ye-	et	wa-	ve
4	5	5	5	4	4	4	3

O'er	the	la-	nd	of	the	free	and	the	home	of	the	brave?
3	3	4	4	5	5	6	4	4	5	5	4	4

The Blues Scale (& Blues Scale Solo Verses)

The *"Blues Scale,"* of course, is the musical alphabet for the Blues, just as the Major and Minor Scales are alphabets for other types of music. My Blues and Rock Breathing Patterns approximate the notes of the Blues Scale — that's why I use them to teach Blues and rock music. But playing an actual Blues Scale requires the technique known as "bending" notes.

About Bending

"Bending" means changing the shape of the inside of your mouth — mostly by using the tongue — which changes the flow of the air going through it. This changes the "pitch" (highness or lowness) of the note. Generally, bending a note means making it sound lower than it normally does.

Your Current Bend Status: Dwahs and Chokes

You've already begun to bend notes to a tiny extent. The dwah effect changes the shape of the inside of your mouth, which gives you the dwah sound. And when you get a "choked" or "funky" 2 in, you are accidently doing a partial bend.

If you can get clean, clear, single in notes, you can try to lower the pitch of a note like this: start, completely empty, on 4 in. Begin the note with your mouth completely relaxed and as open inside as possible. After a second, tighten your tongue and pull it back and down (about an inch). Some people liken this to saying "whee-ooh." If you hear the note change pitch, you're at least on the right track!

It took me ten full months to get my first bend (a 2 in). Now, most people using my *Bending the Blues* method (page 94) get their first bend within a few hours of serious practice spread over several days. Mastering this technique, like so many other things, is the work of a lifetime...

The Simplified Blues Scale and Solo Verse

Even without bending, you can play a version of the Blues Scale that works quite well. Here is the easiest one:

In the third harmonica verse of Playalong Track 22, I use the Simplified Blues Scale to create a solo. Sometimes I just use the scale, from low to high, as in lines one (twice) and in the second half of line two. Other times I create riffs from just a few of the notes of the scale, as in the first half of line two, and line three. I end the verse down low in line four, with a Boogie Woogie variation and a double 1 in for a turnaround.

dwah   dwah   dwah

2 3 4̲ 4 5 6̲   **2 2 3 4̲ 4 5 6̲**

dwah   dwah   dwah

4̲ 3 2   4̲ 3 2   2 3 4̲ 4 5 6̲

dwah   dwah   dwah

4 5 4 5   4̲ 3 2

dwah   dwah   dwah

5 5̲ 4 4̲ 4 slide **1 1**

Using the Simplified Blues Scale

Just work your way up and down the Simplified Blues Scale along with Track 22, play around with the rhythm, and you can't go wrong (or not too far)!

The Real Blues Scale and a Real Blues Solo Verse

Here's the real thing . Notice the bends on the 3 in and the 4 in — the little "**b**" indicates the bend.

2 3ᵦ 4 4ᵦ 4 5 6̇

G Bᵦ C Dᵦ D F G

> This Scale starts and ends on a G note. It is a "Key of G Blues Scale."

In the fourth harmonica verse of Playalong Track 22, I create a solo using this scale — similar to the previous verse, but with bends, and a fancy ending. I've simplified the timing slightly, to make it easier to follow. Want to play like this? My *Instant Blues Harmonica* and *Bending the Blues* will get you there.

2 3ᵦ 4 4ᵦ 4 5 6̇

> Each little "b" tells you to "Bend" that note. A double "bb" tells you to Bend that note really deeply!

2 2 3ᵦ 4 4ᵦ 4 5 6̇

4 34ᵦ 2 34ᵦ 2 4 34ᵦ 2

2 2 3ᵦ 3ᵦ 4 4 4ᵦ 4ᵦ 4 4̲5̲ 34ᵦ 2

4̲5̲ 4̲5̲ᵦ 4̲5̲ 34ᵦ 2
wwwwwwwwwww

dwah

1 2 2 3 2 3 4 3 4 4ᵦ 3 4ᵦ

waaaah wah wah wah

4 slide 1 2 2 2ᵦᵦ (deep bend)

This page is *way* too hard for you to play now — it's only to show you how the Blues Scale is used!

Minor Scale Songs

These songs are all based on the **Minor** Scale of Track 14 (the "musical alphabet" for many wistful or sad songs). As with the Major Scale, many of these songs require "jumps" to avoid missing low notes. Use your wahs, shakes, and dwahs!

Minor Scale Songs — The Missing Notes

Practice the "regular" Minor Scale first, a few times. Then try this new "down and jumping" variation to avoid the low end missing notes. Soon you'll be able to play many Minor Scale based songs, although you may have to "fudge" a note once in a while, as in the "la-a-dy" of *Greensleeves!*

Regular Minor: 4 5̵ 5 6̵ 6 7 7̵ 8

Down and Jumping Minor: 4 4̵ 3 6 6̵ 5 5̵ 4

House of the Rising Sun

There	is	a	house	in	New	Or-	leans	
•	••	•	••	•	••	•	•	•
6	**4**	**4**	**5**	**6**	**6̥**	**4**	**5**	

	they	call	the	ris-	in'	sun	
	•	••	•	••	•	•••	•
	6̥	**6**	**7̵**	**6**	**6̥**	**6**	

And	it's	been	the	ruin	of	this	poor	boy	
•	•	••	•	••	•	••	•	•	•
6	**7̵**	**8**	**8**	**7̵**	**6**	**6̥**	**4**	**5**	

He's	not	the	on-	-	ly	one		No!	
•	••	•	••		•	•••		•	•
5	**4**	**5**	**5̥**	**5**	**5̥**	**45** slide		**6**	

wwww

Saint James Infirm'ry

Went   down   to   Saint James   In   firm   ry

6   **6**   **5**   6   **6**   6   **5**   <u>**45**</u>

Saw   my   ba-   by   was   a   ly   ing   there

5   6   **6**   **6**   **6**   **6**   8   **8**   **6**

Laid   out   on   a   sur-   ge-   ry   ta-   ble

<u>**67**</u>   <u>**67**</u>   <u>**67**</u>   **5**   6   **6**   6   **5**   **4**

So   cold   so   white   so   pa-   le   so   fair

4   **5**   **4**   **5**   <u>67</u>   <u>**67**</u>   <u>67</u>   <u>**56**</u>   <u>**45**</u>

Scarborough Fair (Parsley Sage Rosemary & Thyme)

Are   you   go-   ing   to   Scar-bor-   ough   fair

4   **4**   **6**   6   **5**   **5**   **5**   **5**   **4**

Par-   sley   sage   rose-mar-   y   and thyme

6   7   **8**   7   **6**   **7**   6   **6**

Re-   mem-   ber   me   to   one   who   lives   the-   er-   e

4   **4**   **4**   4   **6**   **6**   6   **5**   5   **4**   4

She   once   was   a   true   love   of   mine

4   **6**   6   **5**   5   **4**   4   **4**

5   **5**   6   **5**   5   **5**   5   4   **4**

Greensleeves

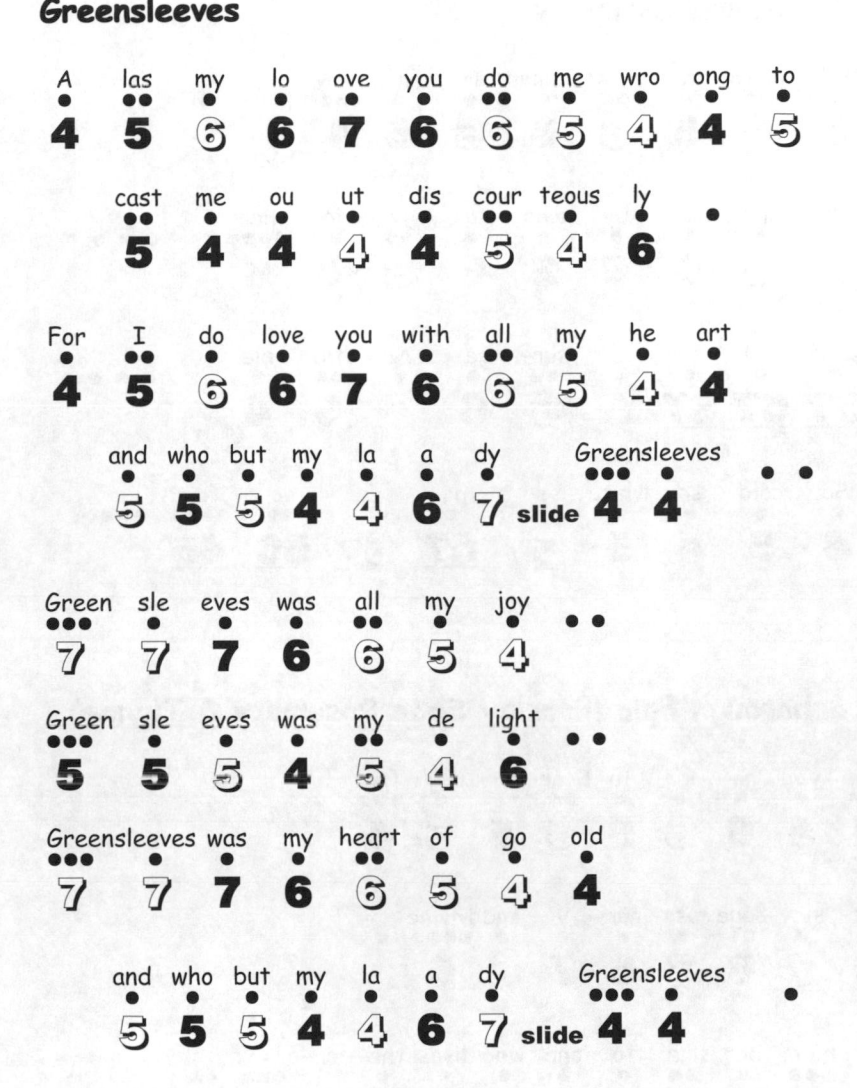

Minor Scale Improvisation

Practice the "regular" Minor Scale on page 46 or page 86 to come up with a Minor improv like the one I play in the background on Track 14 from 1:23 to 1:36. I play the scale going up, then back down, and I end my improv like this:

Another Type of Minor Scale

The next song is based on the "Aeolian" Minor Scale, a variation on the "Dorian" Minor Scale from Track 14. You can play a "non-jump" high version or a lower jumping version that may be more useful in avoiding those pesky missing notes:

High "Non-Jump" Version   **6**   **7**   7̄   **8**   8̄   **9**   9̄   **10**

Low Jumping Version   **6**   6̄   **5**   5̄   **4**   4̄   **7**   **6**

Time to Start Working on "Single Notes?"

The Aeolian Minor Scale will sound best if you can play it with single notes. So if you like this lovely, plaintive, melody, go back to page 52 and put in a few minutes on single noting.

When Johnnie Comes Marchin' Home

When John nie comes mar chin home   a   gain hur ray hur rah
6 5̄ **6** **6** **6** **7** 7̄ **7** 7̄ **6** 6̈ 5̄ 6̈

We'll give 'im   a   rous- in   wel come then hur ray hur rah
6 5̄ **6** **6** **6** **7** 7̄ **7** 7̄ **8** 8̈ **7** 8̈

The men will laugh and   the boys will shout
4̄ 5̄ 5̄ 5̄ **4** 4̄ **4** **4** **4**

The   la   dies the- ey will all turn out
7 7̄ **7** 7̄ **7** **6** **7** **7** **7**

And we'll   all   feel   gay when John nie comes mar chin' home
4̄ **4** 5̄ **4** 4̄ **3** 5̄ **6** **6** **6** 6̄ 6̈

Harmonica Care

Your harmonica is composed of more than 50 separate parts. Attached to the cover plates by rivets are 20 little metal "reeds" — vibrating metal strips — each hand-tuned. Ten of them (the out notes) are on the top cover plate, and ten (the in notes) on the bottom cover plate. Each reed fits into a slot, tight enough so that air can't escape around it, but loose enough so that it can vibrate and make sound.

Reed for 1 in note

Bottom Cover Plate (In notes)

Don't eat and play, unless you're sure there are no food bits to blow into your harmonica. Even a tiny crumb will block a reed from moving, although it can probably be washed out.

Try not to drop it in the mud, but modern (non-wooden) harmonicas can be washed, as long as you rinse all the soap out. *I like to wash a new harp before playing it for the 1st time.*

Don't keep it loose in your pocket — coins or keys get under the cover plates and damage the reeds! Also, hairs can get caught between a reed and its slot, so trim that mustache!

I *do not* recommend removing the cover plates of your harmonica. And *never* touch the reeds — they are delicate!

Want your harmonica to last? Don't play too loudly! Forcing too much air through the reeds makes them go flat (sound lower than they should). When I ask you to play forcefully, that's speaking relatively. Play gentle, soft, folk music and you can use the same harmonica for decades. If you like loud, be prepared to replace your harmonica — a large, loud, rocker may "flatten out" one or more holes of the harp in a single three hour gig, if she blows with all her might....

Note: Why does your harmonica come from China? Because most of the world's low and medium-priced harmonicas do.

Playing Nicely with Others

The material in this method has already prepared you to play some Blues, rock, and folk music on the harmonica — by yourself (actually, with me and my band). Now you're ready to play — or jamm, or *"sit in"* — with other musicians! This is one of the most exciting things a new harp player can do. Knowing *how* to do it will reduce stress and increase pleasure! For more on "Jamming Etiquette," visit *www.bluesharp.com*.

What "Key" Should I Play In?

The "key" of a harmonica refers to the lowest note of that harmonica. The 1 out of your harmonica is a "C" note, so you have a *"harp in the key of C."* But you *won't* always play it in C!

If you only have one harmonica — your "C" harp — that's the key of harmonica you'll use. But the question then arises: "What key should the guitar or band play in?" That depends!

If you're playing a **Major** Scale-based song on your "C" harp, your partners should play in the **key of C** also. This is called, in harmonica jargon: *"Straight Harp"* or playing in *"First Position."*

If you're playing a **Minor Scale**-based song on your "C" harp, your partner or band will need to play in the **key of D minor.** This is called playing in *"Third Position."*

Important: If you are playing **Blues or Rock** using my Breathing Patterns or Riffs on your "C" harmonica, your partner or band should play Blues or Rock in the **key of G.** This is called playing in *"Cross Harp"* or *"Second Position."*

Playing Different Key Harmonicas is Easy!

Harmonicas come in a variety of keys. Generally, "G" is the lowest sounding, and "F" the highest. A new key harp will sound higher or lower, but once you've learned to play your "C" harp, you can *instantly* play *any* song you know on *any* other key harp!

But if you have bought and are using a different key harmonica, then your partners will have to play in different keys, also. The following chart will help. Here's how to use it...

Want to jamm a Blues on your new "B$_b$" harp? (FYI: "$_b$" means "flat.") Find B$_b$ in the top *row* (Harp Key). Go down the B$_b$ *column* to the second row (Blues). Tell your pal to play Blues in the key of F.

If Your **Harp** Key is:	C	D$_b$	D	E$_b$	E	F	G$_b$	G	A$_b$	A	B$_b$	B
Blues or **Rock** Key is:	G	A$_b$	A	B$_b$	B	C	D$_b$	D	E$_b$	E	F	G$_b$
Major Song Key is:	C	D$_b$	D	E$_b$	E	F	G$_b$	G	A$_b$	A	B$_b$	B
Minor Song* Key is:	D	E$_b$	E	F	G$_b$	G	A$_b$	A	B$_b$	B	C	D$_b$

* Each letter in this row represents a minor key, like Dminor, E$_b$minor, etc.

Help for Your Jamming Partners

You can help your jamming partners by telling them which chords to use to play with you. I'll provide a *"chord chart"* (most guitar players are used to these) for one verse of each style of the music you've learned to play from the book and CD.

The Chord Charts (for use when playing with "C" harp only)

Each letter (like "G" or "D7") represents one bar (four beats)* of music. So the chord structure of the Dirty Dog Rock is one bar of G, then one bar of C7, repeated over and over.

Twelve Bar Blues: G-G-G-G-C-C-G-G-D7-C7-G-D7

Twelve Bar Rock: G-G-G-G-C-C-G-G-D7-C7-G-G

Two Bar Two Chord (Dirty Dog) Rock: G-C7

R & B Stress Buster: G/C - D/C (*two beats each chord)

Rock Boogie: Note Pattern is G-G-Bb-C (*one beat each)

All of the Major Songs are in the key of C

Minor Songs are in the key of Dm (D minor) ("When Johnnie" is in A minor)

> Play along with the CD playalong tracks (nice and loud) to keep everyone "on track," especially at first (this is when playing with your key of "C" harp only).

Where to Go From Here (Sales Pitch)

Perhaps it may seem as though I've been giving you a hard sell, suggesting this book or that recording, while all you're trying to do is finish *this* book! If so, I apologize. But I'm painfully aware that this little book only scratches the surface of my favorite topic.

Need to replace the CD that should accompany this book?
Need a "C" harmonica to use with it? Call or email us!

NEW! Jammin' with David: 74 Minute Playalong CD

This CD features me playing in a variety of Blues and rock harmonica styles using a key of C harp. Then it provides you with the same background music *without* my harmonica riffs. So it's easy to hear what I play, then jump to the same track without me, and try it for yourself! A few tracks for key of A and F harps also, plus just a bit of instruction. *$9.95, $2 discount if you buy any other item with it!*

NEW! Mojo Harps in ANY Key, only $7 Each!

NEW! 3 Minutes to Blues, Rock, & Jazz Chromatic!

112 page book, 3 CD set (4 hours long), $24.95. If you play ANY ten hole harp, you'll play blues on chro in minutes! Want more details? Visit www.bluesharp.com and see "New Products!"

Instant Blues Harmonica (9ᵗʰ Edition)

Although quite a bit of the Blues and rock mate-rial in "IBH" is the same as in the book you're holding, *Instant Blues Harmonica* has much more emphasis on understanding how to create impro-vised solos using the Breathing Patterns and the Blues Scale. So if improv appeals to you, it may be worth your while to get this 80 page book/74 minute CD. *Ninth completely revised edition, $14.95.*

Country & Western Harmonica Made Easy

Like country music? You'll be playing along with Shania Twain and Charlie McCoy right away! Some of the material is the same as in the book you're holding, but way more C & W songs and solos are included.
64 page book, 90 minute cassette (sorry, no CD yet), $12.95

Bending the Blues with All NEW 2 CD Set!

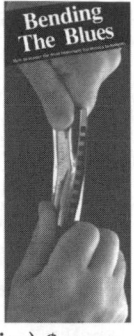

Bending is both the hardest and the most important intermediate harmonica technique. A good "bender" can add up to 16 new bent notes to a standard ten hole harp! This book and 2 CD set (for "C", "A", or "F" harps) *will get total beginners to start bending right away.* It'll then teach you to use ALL draw bends, blow bends, and even "overblows" in a variety of styles, scales, licks, and positions. *Bending book: 64 pages $6.95, 2 CD Set $16.95 Book + 2 CD Set (more than two and a half hours of audio instruction) $22.95*

Bluesmasters Harmonica Classics CD

18 great harp songs by Little Walter, Sonny Boy Williamson II, Jimmy Reed, James Cotton, Paul Butterfield, Jr. Wells, Charlie Musselwhite, Howlin' Wolf, and more! Includes free song-by-song jamming hints/key chart sheet. This and a few harps (C, A, then Bb, then F recommended) will provide you with a lifetime of learning and jamming! *CD $17.95*

Music Theory Made Easy, Deluxe

Not a harmonica book, but a more comprehensive look at music theory for any instrument, and most popular styles. Indispensible for any musician who wants to improvise or play with others. No "reading music" is required! *80 pages, 74 minute CD only $12.95.*

NEW DVD: David Harp's Make Me Musical!

Use David's super easy Harmonica Hand Signal Method™ to play right away! Lots of great extras: playalong songs, PC printable songs, other goodies! *DVD $12.95, with C harp, $17.95).*

Better Breathing Thru Harmonica (Large Print)
Plus methods for Rhythm! Flute! Guitar!

Exercise aerobic capacity with *Better Breathing Through Harmonica (especially for seniors, large print book and Hohner C harmonica $12.95).* Or try one of our great methods for percussion, folk flute (tinwhistle), or the easiest-ever method for guitar. For info on these products, please visit us at our product website: **www.bluesharp.com!**

Last Licks

Enjoyed this harp book?

Try my most important (and internationally best-selling) method: *The Three Minute Meditator,* written with my twin sister Dr. Nina Smiley! New 5th Ed. 256 pp, $14.95, visit *www.thethreeminutemeditator.com*.

Order and Shipping Information

Order Line: 24 hour **1-800-665-6474 (1-800-MOJO-IS-I).** Please have your order ready including: your name, address, items you want sent, credit card number, expiration date, daytime phone and how you want it shipped (described below).

Phone (If you have questions): 802-223-1544 (M-F 10 am-4 pm EST)

Order by email: harpstuf@sover.net (*& request online order form*)

Order by Mail to: Musical i Press 323 South Bear Swamp Rd. Middlesex VT 05602 (Sorry, no COD)

Shipping Costs

Unfortunately, our costs to ship have gone through the roof. We were actually **losing** money when shipping a single $6.95 book! So it's not a misprint that the *more* you order, the *less* it costs to ship!

When Total Cost of Order is:	Order a bit more? We'll pay some of the shipping!			
	Under $10	$10-$25	$25-$50	$50 & UP
These are Ground	$10	$9	$7	$5
shipped 3-day	$13	$12	$10	$8
mostly 2-Day	$15	$14	$13	$11
via Next Day	$25	$24	$23	$22
U.P.S. U.S. Postal Service	$8	$6	$5	$3
Canada*	$9	$7	$6	$4

*By US Post — other countries please write or email for charges.

Order Online & Get Free Gift! www.bluesharp.com

Harmonica player teaches tunes while imparting life's lessons *"it's the most accessible, empowering instrument in the world"*

Man of meditation and music

Pied piper After 20 years of self-doubt and anger, David Harp found peace on the business end of a harmonica.

David Harp: Harmonica phenomenon

Harmonica guru keeps his life in tune

"In his own way, from his little corner of this big ole world, David Harp is doing things to make this a better place to live."
— Charlie Musselwhite, Master Bluesman

The Red, White, and the Blues Harmonica Project

Early in 2003, I began sending free harmonica instruction and harmonicas to people I knew from Central Vermont who were serving in Iraq and Afghanistan. The project expanded rapidly, and with my "RWB" book, CD, & harmonica package I hope to reach many more folk who need the joy, focus, and relaxation that the humble harmonica provides. We make some available free to those serving abroad, and others in bulk at very low cost. For more information, please visit:

www.redwhiteandthebluesharmonica.com

About David and his Work

Many people, especially in the U.S., think of me mostly as a harmonica educator. And I am. But my academic background and training is in psychology, and my passion for the last 15 years has been in the field of *"applied cognitive science."* Huh? Cognitive science is the study of how the neurons and chemicals of the brain produce thoughts and emotions, and how these thoughts and emotions affect our words and actions. "Applied cognitive science" means that I've studied this subject, and want to apply it to real-world situations, at home or work. First to help myself, then to teach others — just as I've done with harmonica.

In the late 1980's I began combining cognitive science *and* harmonica in my work with terminally-ill adults and children, using that strange hybrid to teach stress management and emotional intelligence. It worked so well that I branched out, and for the last five years I've been doing lots of presentations for corporate and non-profit organizations.

My custom events range from a team-creativity workshop for Ben & Jerry's Ice Cream to a workshop on enhancing communication during stressful situations for an international symposium sponsored by the FBI. These unique keynotes and workshops can help *your* organization to work more creatively, more effectively, with better communication and less stress! The money from my corporate work helps subsidize my work with at-risk kids, frail elderly, and people who are terminally-ill, thus I don't mind plugging it here. So if you ever need a corporate speaker... please check out **www.davidharp.com!**

"David was the most popular speaker of our three day event!"
— Carol Evans, Event Co-ordination, American Red Cross